AuthorHouse™ UK Ltd.
500 Avebury Boulevard
Central Milton Keynes, MK9 2BE
www.authorhouse.co.uk
Phone: 08001974150

First published by AuthorHouse 11/17/2008

ISBN: 978-1-4389-2364-2 (sc)

Printed in the United States of America
Bloomington, Indiana

This book is printed on acid-free paper.

authorHOUSE®

FACE READING

How to read the traits of the face

Quick Visual Handbook

BY

RICHARD M PHELAN

PERSONOLOGIST

The scientific study of inherited genetic character traits of the face

To order copies of this book please visit

www.facereading.tv

ISBN 9781438923642

Face Reading – Personology

| Judge Edward Vincent Jones | Dr. Paul B. Elsner PsD Personologist | Robert Whiteside Personologist | Richard M. Phelan Personologist |

Over 60 years of helping people understand who we really are

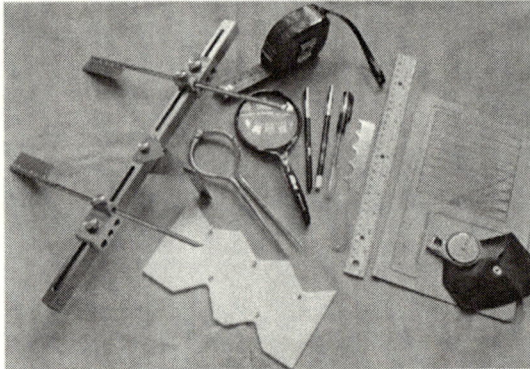

The Face Never Lies

A BRIEF OVERVIEW

Personology for profiling has been used for many years. It has proved to be an invaluable tool in understanding human behaviour, career assessment and relationships. Understanding who you really are by your genetic facial traits has opened up a new outlook on life for many people, as your face never lies. Finding out what your gifts and challenges are has reduced stress in many people's lives, as they now have positive direction and purpose. As regards finding your ideal partner, you will understand that looks, although at first may appear to be important, are not a basis on which to plan a long-term relationship. Understanding the traits of your children and those around you will greatly improve your relationships.

This information is not based on intuitive or psychic readings, but is supported by scientific research and studies over the past 70 years. Controlled studies and investigation programmes make it the most validated method, or system known to date, with 92% accuracy.

The system was discovered by the late USA circuit Judge Edward V Jones USA, validated by personologist Robert Whiteside and further advocated by personologist Dr Paul B Elsner. The system was pioneered and used with excellent results even to the present day.

This book has been prepared to present to the public valuable and accurate information that will be of positive benefit to all who may use this excellent tool. This book uses simple language and explanations that everyone will understand.

Richard M Phelan UK
Personologist

ACKNOWLEDGEMENTS

I should like to express my sincerest thanks to all the people who helped me prepare this book and gave me the opportunity to study their traits so as to be able to produce a book illustrating how we can understand who we are by our facial traits.

I have been able to prepare this book due to my studies and research for which I am truly grateful to USA personologist and face language expert Naomi Tickle. She gave me so much help at the beginning. Thanks also to the late Dr Paul B Elsner, who gave me his time and shared his knowledge, passing on to me a lot of information. Also to the late Robert Whiteside, who spent many years validating the system, establishing its accuracy in profiling and giving constructive help to so many, working alongside Judge Edward V Jones with regard to the US penal institutions and correction facilities for offenders.

My sincere thanks and gratitude to Phil Cook without whose help I could not have prepared the art- and technical work.

Thanks also to all those who gave me their support and encouragement over the years, in research and experiences. Not forgetting my wife Edna, who has given me 100% support while preparing this information with her happy temperament.

My heartfelt thanks to the many people who patiently let me photograph and interview them. Sadly hundreds of photos, for practical reasons, could not be included in the book.

After years of requests and much research, I am happy to say I finally prepared the book so many of you kept asking me for. I hope all will enjoy reading it and use the knowledge enclosed. It is a wonderful tool for all.

Foreword

This book has been prepared to help people, and those around them, understand who they are so as to be able to communicate and improve relationships. We live in a world full of technology and gadgets, with super high-speed broadband computers, email, mobile phones, text messaging, yet the age-old problem still remains – we cannot communicate with each other, simply because we do not understand ourselves or those we come in contact with. Soap operas are, for example, typical of many scenes where people argue, fight, squabble and bicker over mundane things: where we constantly see people falling out with each other due to misunderstanding causing disunity. Although this may be only on TV, it reflects people as they really are. This is the image that is impressed and instilled in the minds of viewers and put upon the young generation who grow up thinking this is the normal way of life. It is not.

It is therefore vitally necessary, if we are to survive in peace and make domestic, family and community living a happy endeavour, that we be educated in the basic understanding of human behaviour and why we may be drawn to do or react to the things we do. It is hoped that as you read these pages, they will open a door of understanding on who you really are; what your potential is and what your gifts and talents that maybe you never realised you had. You will never look at a face the same way again. You will understand yourself and others – why you do certain things and behave in a certain way. You will discover both your gifts and challenges and how to bring out the very best in yourself and others.

Contents

AREA THREE: Action Traits

AREA FOUR: Feelings and Emotion Traits

AREA FIVE: Thinking Traits

QUICK REFERENCE AND INDEX

HOW TO USE THIS BOOK
– a wonderful tool

The subject of face reading is an interesting observation tool, is very valuable and should be enjoyable to use. The traits are divided into five areas, as you will soon learn from this book. After each trait area section we have left a few pages for your personal notes or to stick personal photos. You will be able to use these pages many times. We recommend that you get a light pencil and write down the facial features of people you know or meet. Then, by making a note of the main features, you can flick through the book, using the index at the back to find the correct information about their facial features. For example, the boss –

My boss has...slim face,
eyes close together, and deep-set,
protruding chin,
a Roman-type nose and
his ears tend to stick out...

You can look up each section and build up a picture of who he really is. This will give you the great advantage of knowing exactly how to approach him...especially when you want to ask for that next pay rise! Remember, education is serious but it should be enjoyable to learn. So take a look at your friends and family, then compare what you observe of their facial traits with the information contained here. You will be amazed by what you will learn. If you see people arguing or conflicting look at their facial traits and see if you can understand why they conflict. With your new knowledge you will be able to handle almost anyone, as you will now understand who they really are and why they do the things they do. Your communication with others will greatly increase and should be very successful, with few conflicts.
Think of this book like your mobile phone, take it everywhere with you and use it!

WHAT IS PERSONOLOGY?

Personology is the scientific study of reading inherited genetic traits of the face so as to be able to understand who we really are and human behaviour. For those in a relationship, the good news is…

you can live together in peace without murder!

Personology (also known as face reading) for profiling has been used for many years. It has proved to be an invaluable tool for understanding human behaviour, career assessment and relationships. Understanding who you really are by your genetic facial traits has opened up a new outlook on life for many people, as your face never lies. Finding out what your gifts and challenges are has reduced stress in many people's lives as they now have a positive direction and purpose. With regards to finding your ideal partner, you will understand that looks, although at first may appear to be important, they are no basis on which to plan a long-term relationship. Understanding the traits of your partner, children and those around you will greatly improve your relationships. This information is not based on intuitive or psychic readings but is supported by scientific research and studies over the past 70 years. Controlled studies and investigation programmes make it the most validated system known to date. If you doubt this, study your face and compare the contents of each section with yourself. You will be truly amazed what you will discover about yourself and others!

People are like phone numbers!

The best way to illustrate and explain inherited genetic facial traits is by considering the basic principle of numbers. We have, in the UK, for example, 10 digits including a zero. All telephone numbers are made up from these 10 digits, yet we have millions of different phone number combinations; no two phone numbers are the same. Likewise, every human has 68 basic facial traits, and there are about 20 additional environmental traits. For example, over a long period of time some people develop a down-turned mouth due to disappointment, when in fact all children are born with an up-turn mouthed. As no two people have the same combination of traits, where one person has a strong, or high score, trait in one area, another has a low score. By looking at these traits and seeing which of these, for example, in a cluster is more dominant, we can begin to see the pattern of the character develop. Although similar, no two individuals have an identical personality and are as unique as a fingerprint. Genetic testing and profiling through personology provides another tool to unlocking the knowledge of who we really are and family inherited traits.

No two telephone numbers are the same...

Uncle Ted	01367 896543
Cousin Jill	03367 014444
Granddad	22887 622991
Bob	39401 347599
My Boss	88591 233455

Although we may share similarities, we are all individually as unique as our finger prints. There are no two identical faces on the planet...or the universe!

Six generations of traits

We all inherit six generations of traits and pass on five to our children. The child's own traits make up another six and so on. Some traits are suppressed and lost and new traits may surface if refined, enhanced or cultivated. By looking at family photos, you will see these traits; some strong in some members and some stronger in others. Also, by looking back through the father's family line and the mother's family line, you will see where the gifts and challenges you have inherited from your traits may have come from.

FACE READING –
A WONDERFUL TOOL FOR ALL

Reading facial traits
The system used, in keeping up-to-date with scientific progress, is modern in its approach. It was "discovered" by Judge Edward Vincent Jones. After watching people standing before him in his Los Angeles court for many years, he found he could predict their behaviour from their facial features or traits. He was so fascinated by his discovery that he started keeping detailed notes. From his records he realised he was describing a new science which he termed "personology". Previously similar studies were known as "physiognomy". This was a new approach to reading facial traits. The system required detailed validation to be accepted as reliable, and this is exactly what Judge Jones undertook with the help of Robert Whiteside.

Proving the system
Jones shared his discovery and his records with Robert Whiteside, a newspaper editor in San Francisco. Whiteside was impressed with the accuracy and immediately saw the value of Jones's work for real, human situations. Whiteside set up detailed tests with a group of 1,050 adults – enough to get an accurate statistical validation. The result was 92% accurate. Robert Whiteside carried out some 15,000 one-to-one personal consultation profiles, some for criminal investigation with amazing accuracy and results, many within the penal system such as San Quinton prison.

Avoid misunderstanding and attain better communication
- Understand who you really are and what your facial traits mean.
- Discover your gifts and what possible challenges you might face in life.
- Know immediately how the person you are talking to will react.
- Know how to assign the right person the correct job.
- Know exactly how much information to give to any individual.
- Understand your partner and why you may conflict.
- Avoid misunderstandings in dealing with others.
- Understand your children, and their learning abilities.

12

Avoid misunderstanding and attain better communication

Continued:

- Find your perfect partner and never argue.
- Understand the six basic traits for an ideal partner.
- Understand mood swings and the root cause.

Is face reading another "forer" effect? Why we say "NO"

What is "the forer effect"

The forer effect, or the subjective evaluation effect, is "that people tend to accept vague and general personality descriptions as uniquely applicable to themselves, without realizing that the same description could be applied to just about anyone." Horoscopes and all sorts of personality tests, among many other methods, depend on this effect to seem valid. Case studies have shown that many so-called experts used this technique to win over unsuspecting, vulnerable individuals.

Such a manner, or type of reading, is also called "cold reading". Cold reading refers to a set of techniques used by professional manipulators to get a subject to behave in a certain way or to think that the cold reader has some sort of special ability that allows him to "mysteriously" know things about the subject.

Personology does not follow or agree with using this type of blind approach to profiling. A good personologist will look at the trait and measure in detail and chart the score. If personology is used then we have to consider that each and every person is different. Photos taken can show the traits and allow the individual to see for himself where or how the final results come from. Seeing we are all different, it is unlikely that any two people will have exactly the same profile reading. It is for this reason that we invite you all to consider the information presented in this book, not blindly accepting what we have stated but to put it to the test.

The accuracy of so many traits set genetic profiling apart from many of the holistic-type readings so common today. It is also wrong to assume that just because a person has a trait or set of traits in a facial area, they can automatically be judged and labelled as a specific type of person. To explain this, we can look at the example of a man who has a set of tools in his garage and a pile of timber. This does not mean he has a new piece of furniture. It means he has the potential of having it. It all depends on what he decides to make and when, and if he ever gets around to making it!

Likewise, it's up to each individual how he uses his traits. One man might have great potential to be an excellent surgeon and be very skilful with his hands, but if he decides he prefers to go to the gym and punch the life out of an opponent in a boxing ring, that's his decision. He will never become the highly-skilled surgeon he could have been. We all have many gifts and great potential. What we present here is the knowledge so you can look at yourself and see how to cultivate the very best in you and bring out the very best of your traits, producing for you happiness and a better and meaningful life.

It is unwise to assume that personology is "THE tool" best used to understand people. There are many tools and excellent counsellors in their field around today. What we present here is another tool which, by combining the knowledge that each one can contribute, we can draw off each others experiences and expertise. Together we can reveal the secrets of what we search for as an answer. What one man may miss another will find: what one man may lack another may excel in. A carpenter doesn't use just one tool, such as a hammer, but many tools. The more tools we have access to, the greater the chance of producing good results.

AN IDEAL TOOL
FOR SPECIAL SERVICES

- Police and public order organizations.

- Security and airport staff training.

- Those working with offenders and institutions.

- Lawyers and those working within the court system.

- Social services and relationship counselling.

- Marriage guidance counselling agencies.

- Marketing and sales training.

- Business communication and customer service training.

- Education and schools.

- Career assessment and human resources agencies.

- Domestic help organizations.

- Dating agencies and partner matching.

THE BENEFITS OF HAVING THE KNOWLEDGE OF FACE READING

- **Teachers** – you will be able to identify your students' learning and thinking style. Quickly recognize which traits are holding them back and what is causing a problem.

- **Coaches** – you will be able to recognize which traits keep your clients from moving forward and the ones that create their greatest challenges. You'll also find out more about their gifts.

- **Sales people** – immediately identify your clients' thinking and buying process.

- **Parents of adopted and foster children** - knowing your child's strengths and challenges will help you understand better and work with them, turning negative traits into gifts.

- **Relationships** – discover which traits will create challenges in a relationship, and know if a person is your perfect partner, before making that all-important commitment of " I DO!"

- **Human resources departments** – contracting the right person for the correct position in your company.

- **Personal development** – knowing more about your own traits, and those of your family, friends and work colleagues, will help you avoid much of the miscommunication experienced at work and in domestic situations.

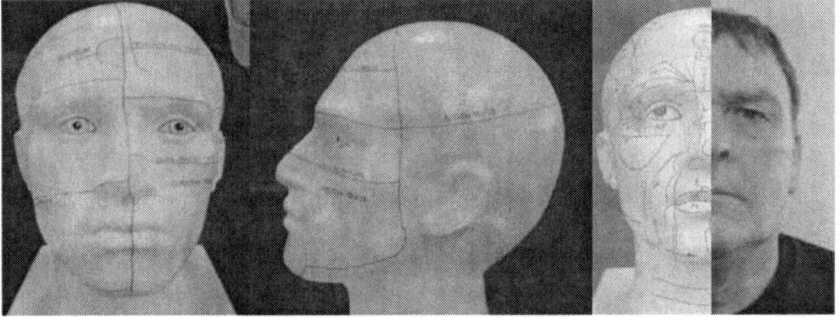

Facial trait areas of the head and face.

HOW TO START TO READ A FACE

To learn how to make a very quick observation and give someone the "once over", as they say, here are a few tips to get you started. The traits of the face are divided into five trait areas. Learn the basic five areas then pick out the most dominant traits in that area. If you can pick out just one or two traits from each area, you will very quickly build a picture of who the person really is and have a pretty good idea how they will react and what they will do. Each of the trait areas is explained in the book. They are:

1 Physical traits,
2 Automatic traits,
3 Action traits,
4 Emotion and feeling traits,
5 Thinking traits.

You will, by quick observation, then know:

- How sensitive the person is
- What they will automatically be inclined to do
- What drive they have, positive or a procrastinator etc
- How they will approach situations
- How the person thinks and handles information and situations

Once you practice this and master these very basic steps, you will be truly amazed that a short time spent gaining experience will really help you in dealing with those you come in contact with in any given situation. You may wish to start to collect your own photos from magazines or relatives and build up your own photo library so as to study and use them to help others.

THE FIVE TRAIT AREAS

There are 68 basic traits of the face and at least 20 additional environmental traits. These traits are also divided into five areas. There are no bad traits: there are only good traits and traits that are sometimes out of control. Certain traits will tend to take control and become dominant in an area. If these traits are not guided into a positive direction they will control the person rather than the person having control of his traits. Knowing which traits affect certain behaviour patterns, we are able to take the necessary precautions to help turn our negative traits into positive gifts. If we have more than one trait which can be a gift or challenge, giving us the desire to go in a certain direction, these are called "trait clusters".

The five trait areas are:

Area one: Physical Traits
These are found in hair thickness, leg length, hand dexterity, for example, length of fingers etc. Physical traits such as thickness of hair and leg length greatly influence us in what we do so one should carefully consider these traits when selecting a partner, as they play a major part in compatibility between couples.

Area two: Auto Expression Traits
These identify how people will automatically react to situations and handle them, and how they confront issues when they arise. Traits are found in the lower part of the face. The area is from the nose to the bottom of the chin.

Area three: Action Traits
These force and drive us to move on any decision or project. Action traits are the most powerful and will be the negative or positive drive to all the other traits. Action traits determine the force and drive for certain things whereas emotional traits govern what we choose to be driven toward or driven by. The traits are found at the top, side and rear of the head.

Area four: Feelings and Emotions Traits
These identify how sensitive we are toward others. They determine what we choose to be driven by or the desire by which we're motivated. The more emotional the person the more they will let emotion guide their thinking rather than logic. Sometimes basic commonsense may be pushed aside. The traits are found in the top part of face, particularly the eye area.

Area five: Thinking Traits
How we process information and why we may conflict with others for no apparent reason come into this area. These traits reveal not only how we process information, but also our response to information received and how we tend to handle it. Schoolteachers, particularly, will find this information very helpful in dealing with students. In the education system, at times a negative attitude toward children comes from lack of understanding on the part of the teacher, who doesn't realize the child's traits for thinking and processing information, and this is not the child's fault at all. A huge leap forward can be made when this knowledge of an individual's thinking process is understood. It can avoid much frustration and conflict. The traits are found mainly in the forehead area of the head. A list of traits, and how they can affect children at school, is printed at the back of the book and contributed by Dr Paul B Elsner's work.

When a child is learning to play an instrument, he/she will play some wrong notes. These notes are not bad, by no means; they are just wrong notes that they play at the wrong time or place. Traits are also like this. If they are out of control or lack direction, they will be at the root of many problems. Using the very same traits, in both a positive and constructive way, we can turn what was once a challenge and negative influence in one's life, into a wonderful gift with very good, positive results.

There are no bad traits…
    …there are good traits…
        …and traits that are out of control

AREA ONE: PHYSICAL TRAITS

LEG LENGTH AND TORSO LENGTH

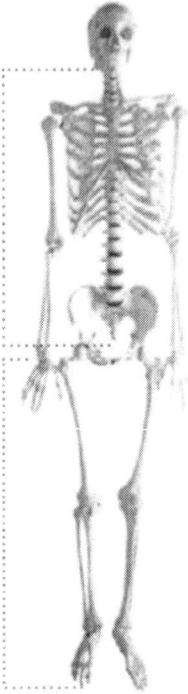

MATERNAL
Long body short leg.
Takes after the mother

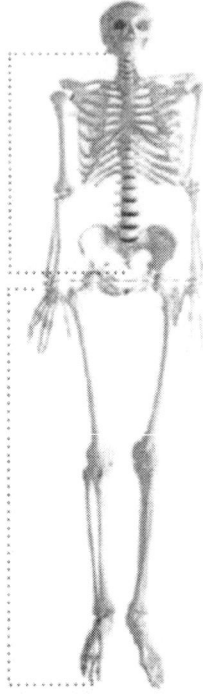

PATERNAL
Short body long leg.
Takes after the father

Who do you take after, your mother or your father?

We inherit half our traits from our mother and half from our father. By measuring the torso and the length of the legs we can determine which of our parents is the dominant one in our inherited traits. If we are right-handed then the dominant parent is our right side. If we are left-handed then the dominant parent is our left side. All we need to know is which parent is it? This can be confirmed very easily. If the torso is short and the legs are longer than the torso, this is called "paternal" (after the father). If the torso is long and the legs are shorter then this is "maternal" (after the mother). Some teenagers appear to be all legs and feet as well as very clumsy when growing up and resemble grasshoppers when they sit down, with legs and knees going in every direction! Once they stop growing, dominance is easy to determine.

Shorter-legged people are more active: longer-legged people are more inclined to sit at desk jobs. Even if interested in sport, individuals will vary in the choice of activity. Problems arise when couples, for example, have more than an average difference especially when extreme. When this occurs one partner will want, for example, to travel by car; the other will want to walk. One will want to rest often and recover, while the other will continue to be on the move. They can become irritated with the other partner continually needing rest. Short-legged people always like to be on the move and on the go.

Can I sit behind that long-legged man?

People who appear to look the same height may, in fact, be a different height when they sit down, due to the difference in torso length or length of the spine. So, if you have to sit behind someone in a theatre or cinema, sit behind a long-legged person, as these will tend to have a shorter torso and you will get a better view!

Although this may appear to be an insignificant factor in a relationship, it is in fact very important. Disagreements, even heated arguments, can erupt due to impatience when one has a partner with longer legs who cannot keep up with a shorter-legged partner who always likes to be on the go. Longer-legged people prefer to rest often and use transport rather than walk. When all is said and done, the more the leg lengths match in a partnership, the fewer problems and conflict of interests will occur when it comes to travel, sports and such like activities.

Are they an ideal partner?

Check out the legs. Most men do, but now they have another reason for looking!

LEGS AND CAREERS

When considering a career the legs play an important role. For long-legged people to stand on their feet all day will be quite a challenge. This is why most office workers are more inclined to be long-legged as they do tend to prefer desk jobs and sitting down most of time. People with long legs need to remember that they still need to exercise even if they feel they'd prefer to sit back in a chair. If a job requires you to spend a lot of time on your feet, then it is best to take frequent breaks and, as they say, put your feet up. Long-legged people find standing for long periods of time rather stressful and demanding.

Some people have long legs yet are very restless. If this is the case, it will be due to an over-riding trait in the lower part of the face called "physical motive". This is explained later in the book. It's for this reason that, if a person has long legs and he can't stay put or wants to be on the move all the time (for example, a child at school who will not stay in his seat), you will find the cause is usually that the child has a dominant trait called "physical motive", which is in the "automatic trait" area of the face. The automatic trait will tend to be the first one to lead the person in a direction with other traits taking second place.

Shorter legged people on the other hand will stand on their feet all day and will be constantly on the move. If you have been given a desk job, this may be challenging, so again frequent breaks are the answer as being confined to a chair for hours on end will be quite an ordeal. Employers wanting to recruit personnel should look at this information and carefully choose who is best suited for the job. It might be, as some have found out, that to study your employees' traits and simply move them around has resulted in more efficient and productive results and happier employees!

HAIR THICKNESS, SKIN, BODY TONE, SENSITIVITY

HAIR THICKNESS

Hair thickness is the person's sensitivity. We call it the body insulation or temperament. The finer the hair the more sensitive the person is (Fig A following pages). The coarser the hair the more it takes to upset them. We often refer to people as being thick skinned (Fig B). The difference is like two people going for a walk on a freezing cold morning. One has a thick warm coat while the other has a short-sleeved, thin, cotton shirt. The thicker the hair or insulation the greater the resistance to outside elements that could affect them or upset them. Coarse-haired people tend to be tougher: they love the outdoor life and don't let things upset them, although underneath they could be very sensitive. Finer haired people will tend to get upset easily. In some people, if one side of the head has fine hair and other side has coarse hair, this is caused by asymmetry in traits, due to two very different parents. In some cases it will cause serious mood swings in sensitivity and response to others.

We often see celebrities and sports personalities who have thick, course hair, choosing a partner with the opposite. Let's say, for example, a man chooses a woman with baby-fine hair who looks sexy and feminine. Yet eventually they split up and part. Why? The first attraction is that he is tough, strong and manly while she is warm, sensitive, gentle and very feminine. But as time goes by, he will feel she is too sensitive, gets upset and hurt too easily and cries over things. He feels she is just a baby and loses patience with her. She thinks he is insensitive and doesn't consider her feelings enough – is unkind and not thoughtful toward her.

But what is the real problem? Simply, they do not match. In this case a course-haired female would have no problem handling such a man and would not find his attitude offensive. A finer haired man would be very sympathetic to the woman's feelings and be very gentle and responsive toward her.

HAIR THICKNESS

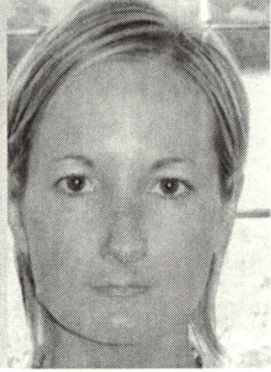

Fig A	Fig B	Fig C
Fine hair more sensitive	Course or thick hair tougher temperament	Tight skin clinical look, more fussy and picky

Fig D   Fig E

Sensitivity and body tone

If she is a fine-haired woman, she will like softer music, more refined food, and quieter surroundings and speak with more tact. She would want to stay in five to seven star hotels, not rough it in a tent or camping in a field. Children, particularly with baby-fine hair, can be very finicky eaters and have the same manner in adulthood. As a child, these types of people could be given a stuffed pea and a leg of mouse to eat and they will still leave something on the side of the plate! A course-haired man will be loud in many of his manners such as talking. He will like louder music, be rougher in sports, appear less considerate and sometimes arrogant or obnoxious, almost to the point of being undesirable to be around at times. He will like noisy cars, do heavy work such as construction, drive trucks and machinery and have interests like mountain climbing, exploring etc. He will have an appetite that would put a horse to shame. He will eat big meals such a cow pie, a huge stack of potatoes and vegetables, generally appearing insensitive toward others.

Most politicians have course hair, which is why they appear insensitive and unsympathetic. In some cases they are! Fine-haired people like quality, course or thick haired people like quantity. If you are looking for a partner check out their hair first. The place to check is on the side of the head just in front of the ear. Personologists use a instrument such a paper thickness tool to measure hair which can be from 1,000th of an inch to 5,000th of an inch. 1,000th to 2,000th would be sensitive and fine hair, 2,000th to 3,000th medium and 4,000th or above would course hair.

As mentioned already, when a child has a parent with fine hair and another with course or thick hair, that child may be found to have different thicknesses: one side of the head has fine while the other side has thick or course hair. In this situation, you will see mood swings which can be mild to extreme. On one occasion they may sit happily in a hall listening to a live band, while on another occasion will want to walk out and feel they cannot stand the noise. This may also be true of some who may wish to rough it on a camping holiday but the next time complain over every little issue leaving the family with no ideas why. In such situations, people with a mood swing in this area do well to always remember to do things in moderation and not to put themselves in extreme situations. They can make themselves feel very uncomfortable, much to the confusion of people around them who do not understand their change of behaviour, or why the individual suddenly changes his or her mind about what he or she is doing. In relationships the hair thickness is the number one trait to consider for compatibility and something that, no matter how much you may feel attracted to the individual, can spell possible future disaster if you ignore this fact. Trust me!

THE SKIN

The skin is also an indication of the type of person the individual is. Observation reveals some interesting things about skin. People with what might be said to be tight skin over the face and forehead (Fig C) have what we call the clinical look. They are found to be far more picky and fussy in everything. The looser the skin over the head and face the more lax the person will be and less fussy, most likely in all areas of their life. This also applies to people who appear to have more rounded or what might be termed as "blunt" features. Those with tight skin as well as having sharper features will often be seen working in beauty, health, medical positions and such like. Those with a looser type skin are prone to be messy, untidy, less fussy and more laid back.

This is a good exercise to do. Just make a list of everyone you know and then study their traits and compare them with what you learn from this book. You will be amazed by what you will see and learn. Look at the skin then compare how they live at home and what they do for employment – you may be surprised what you find!

BODY TONE

As with hair thickness and skin tone, body tone will also reflect a person's nature pretty accurately. Soft muscle tone and more fragile-looking build will tend to reflect a person who is softer by nature – sensitive, gets hurt or offended easily and is more emotional (Fig E). Whereas a person with a body tone that is of harder muscle and build will tend to come across as insensitive, unsympathetic and with less emotion. They will be what we call tough guys (Fig D). People who are softer by nature need to toughen up, so going to the gym can do a power of good, give a feeling of confidence and building stamina. The voice also will reflect a person. A sharp or loud voice will come across as being authoritative and will exert power. A gentle, soft or quieter voice, on the other hand, will reflect a person who is more inclined to be thoughtful, kind and sensitive in dealing with others. In some cases, people who are extremely sensitive and shy will come across as if whispering when talking.

Body tone will reflect a person's temperament and sensitivity, depending on whether they are of a tougher nature or if they are more inclined to be sensitive to people, the environment and situations. Look at the illustrations here and study the people around you, and ask yourself "if they spoke, what type of voice or tone do you think they will have?" Pure observation will give you a pretty good idea. Put it to the test!

Keeping peace and harmony

None of us are perfect, and in a working environment keeping peace and harmony is very important. It is so important to realise that no progress can be made until peace and harmony is agreed and achieved right from the start. If for some reason you find that you clash with another, it may be because there is a subtle, but important difference in hair thickness between family, friends, employees or even a boss.

A course-haired person, put in charge of several fine-haired people, will most likely come up against a number of issues due to his harder presentation of himself, resulting in others feeling uncomfortable having to deal with such a person. On the other hand, a sensitive, fine-haired person in a position of authority may find he is the object of ridicule, taunting or abuse due to those under him being of a courser nature and poking fun at him.

Feelings of hurt, embarrassment and resentment can all be corrected if everyone is given the correct information about those they work with and their traits. It is for this reason that employers should spend a little time understanding employees' traits which can really bring the best out of all, contributing to a healthy, happy environment and resulting in a more progressive and successful business. As they say, a happy job is a successful job. Any conflict, no matter how small, can seriously affect production and a business.

No one would expect to see a carpenter using medical instruments to do a job, nor a surgeon using tools of a brick layer. Yet this is what we find in many companies. They have great tools, but they are often used for the wrong jobs. Success in business is based on using the right tools (or people) in the best possible positions of the business or doing the job best suited to them. Biblical ancient King Solomon wrote these words witnessing the same problem:

"I have seen servants on horses but princes walking the earth like servants". **Ecclesiastes chapter 10 verse 7.**

THE HANDS

Very good hand dexterity   Also good dexterity

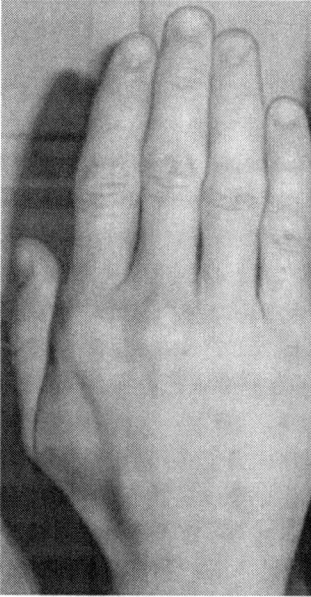 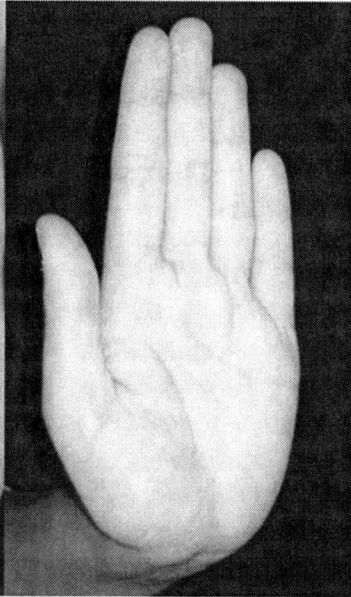

Fig A   Fig B

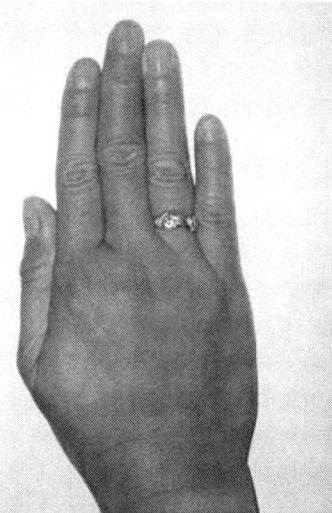 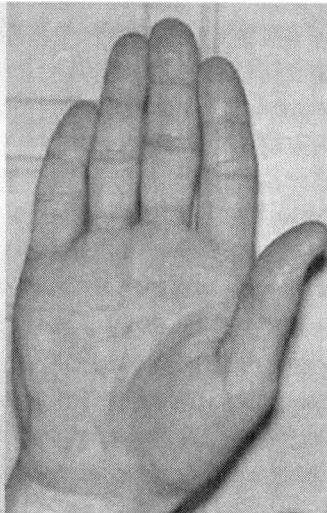

Fig C
Risk taker

Fig D
Philosophical

HAND DEXTERITY, RISK-TAKING, PHILOSOPHICAL, EXPLOSIVE EMOTIONS, SOLITUDE

It's amazing that people with exceptionally large hands are often gifted to do the most nimble and delicate of jobs especially crafts. The reason why can be seen by a close examination of the length of the fingers. People whose fingers are almost the same length, as in example Fig A, appear to have more ability in hand dexterity and are gifted to use their hands, especially for playing instruments and doing the tiniest of jobs. Fig B, also showing the first finger almost equal to the second finger, usually belong to people with very good hand dexterity, gifted, especially in art and crafts, and usually very neat writers. People with even finger length also give a great massage! This doesn't mean that people with odd finger lengths can't use their hands well; it simply means they will find that they have to work that little bit harder to master it.

In Fig C, you will notice the ring finger is longer than the first finger. When we see this trait it is an indication of a risk taker. These can be physical risks, financial risks or whatever the other dominant traits are. If they are adventurous, it will amplify the trait. People with a high risk-taking trait do things just for the fun and thrill of it – they like the excitement, the buzz, no matter what the dangers are. People with thin lips, low tenacity and low impulsiveness will be more inclined to be "calculated risk takers". They weigh everything up and then go in for the kill, so to speak. Those with high tolerance, impulsiveness and tenacity will be more impulsive risk takers. "Do it now, think later" is their motto! If the trait is found on only one hand there will be a mood swing in this area: they will take a risk one day; the next they will hold back.

If they have a number of traits which follow a behaviour pattern, this is what is termed a "trait cluster". An example would be a person with high tolerance, objective thinking or fast thinking, ears flat to the head (indicating a quick spender), forward balance (likes to move forward on things) , forcefulness and competitiveness. All these traits can be found in individuals who like to gamble. A person with such traits would be highly competitive, an impulsive risk-taker and would certainly have an attitude of "do now, and think later". Parents having children with risk-taking traits do well to direct them into sports and activities that guide the desire for excitement in a constructive direction. Otherwise, they will seek the excitement in pursuits that can lead to crime due to frustration.

On a humorous note, regarding hands, one man was told when applying for a job *"We are very sorry sir, we cannot offer you a job as a waiter, your hands are far too big and you make our meals look very small."*

PHILOSOPHICAL

An interesting trait, also seen in many people, is "philosophical trend" (Fig D). This is identified by the gaps between the fingers, when the fingers are closed together which looks as if they have bony fingers. In fact, some people have quite thick fingers yet still have this trait. This is an innate desire towards spiritual or higher thinking. They like to ask questions "why are we here?"; "is there a God?" They seem to always be on a quest for life, searching for the meaning of things. They like meditation and relaxing soft music and peace, seeking to find out about their higher self. Many young people, especially men who have this trait, are pulled into religious cults. (There are over 5,000 religious cults in the USA.) They are taken in by mind-control methods used to lure them in, only to find they become slaves to a religious system they find hard to leave.

People who are philosophical tend to set the ball rolling. They initiate the first step, being highly philosophical – questioning and willing to learn from their searches anything that might be the answer. The warning is given if you have this trait. Beware, as there are many religious cults willing to take you in, take your money and time and offer nothing in return. It was observed that a large number, who died at the "Heavens Gate" religious cult incident in the USA, had this trait.

INTENSE FEELINGS, EXPLOSIVE EMOTIONS

This trait is seen when an individual has exceptionally long thumbs. Again, if they have this on one hand only, there will be a mood swing with the trait. The trait is made obvious by tendency to explosive emotions often called "intense feelings". Caution needs to be taken to ensure this is measured correctly. *The hand should be laid completely flat.* This can be done by putting your hand flat against a window or pane of glass. The palm must be flat against the surface…remember, NO CHEATING! From this you will be able to see if you have this trait. It's not that common, but the tip of the thumb will appear to be level with the first finger joint or a little longer. It's of interest to note that this is mostly found as a genetic trait in the Irish. It manifests itself when a person suddenly displays an explosive outburst in temper, feelings or great excitement. They roar up, much to the surprise and shock of bystanders, and then calm down and carry on as normal as if nothing had happened. It's a sort of heat of the moment reaction outburst.

Parents with this trait should be cautious not to lash out at siblings or their partners in the heat of the moment, as many a hole has been punched through a door or wall in an uncontrolled, explosive outburst. Men who have this trait should consider sports such as throwing the shot, discus, javelin, rowing, weights and power lifting. They will have a naturally explosive energy that will leave others standing. Woman likewise should seek explosive-type sports to help release the energy and bring the trait under control. A display of champions' trophies looks so much better on the shelf than holes punched in the doors and walls of your home. Trust me!

SOLITUDE LINE

For those who like to study their palms or are interested in palm reading, here is an interesting trait. A short headline, when looking at the palms of your hand, is an indication of those who need time to themselves. These people will willingly work, entertain and socialize with others, but they must have their time alone. It has also been termed "the hermit line", as those who hide or lock themselves away like hermits and enjoy isolation tend to have this trait. People with a longer headline usually like to have company and enjoy being surrounded by friends and family, all hours of the day. In other words, people with this trait like to have their own space. Marriage partners of people with this trait should not feel hurt or offended if one party says "I want to be on my own for while" and locks themselves in the workshop or elsewhere to enjoy some recreation for themselves. They like to have time to themselves – to think, relax and basically be alone to find their peace. Once they have this time to themselves, they are happy to carry on as normal.

MELANCHOLY AND DEPRESSION

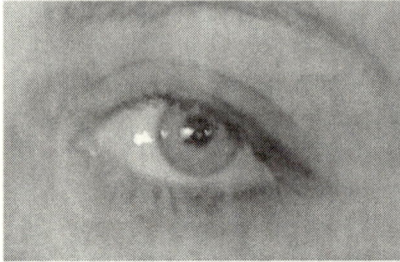 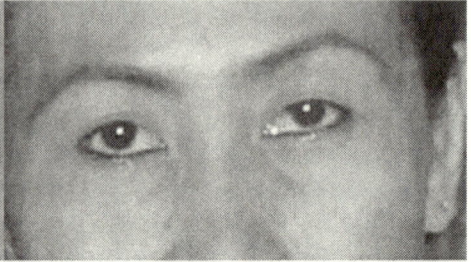

Fig G   Fig H

Fig J

Melancholy is indicated by white under one or both irises of the eyes. If under one eye, it will manifest itself in being accident-prone. If there is white under both eyes, it is a sign of serious long or ongoing stress and depression.

The eyes are the window of the inner soul or feelings. No matter what a person says, it's all there in the eyes. When looking at a person face on, seeing white under one or both eyes (clearly visible in Fig G, H and J) is a sign of "melancholy" or serious depression caused by severe stress, long-term depression or trauma. Eyelids may appear to drop slightly as if giving a tired look. People suffering from this are likely to be accident prone, they may also appear glassy-eyed if under stress (called "fugacity") or appear bloodshot. If this is the case, they really should not be driving any type of vehicle or operating machinery as they are a high risk factor and a danger to themselves as well as others. They should seek help and establish what is the real cause of the problem, as it has obviously been going on for some time, and take steps to rectify a problem seriously affecting their life. As a person starts to alter his/her life and thinking, the face will relax and the eyelids will return to normal.

Melancholy and signs of stress were rarely seen in children at one time, yet today it is very common. While researching this, it was disturbing to see so many young people suffering, as it is an indication that many young people are extremely unhappy in their home lives. If a parent starts to see this sign in their child, they should take prompt action to seek the cause and solve the problem as soon as possible. Individuals suffering melancholy can be an accident waiting to happen, especially if allowed to drive any sort of vehicle or even a bicycle.

THE NECK – VOCAL LINES

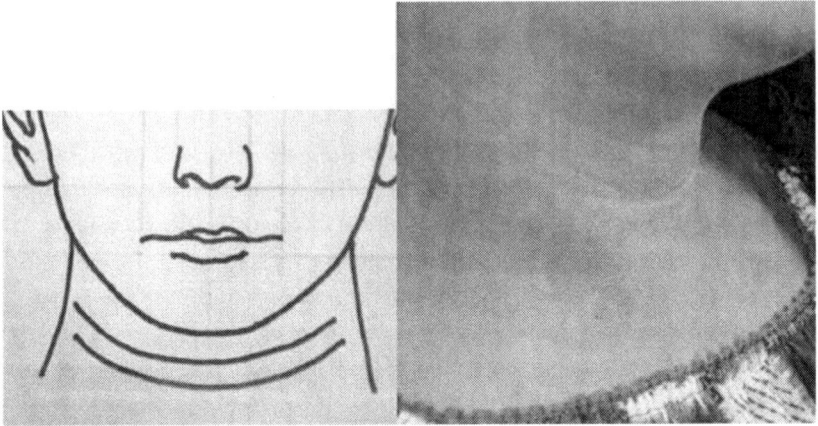

Two lines across front of the neck are known as "vocal lines". People with this trait show they are gifted with potential singing ability. Children who have this trait should be encouraged to sing. If they also have music ability (see information under the section discussing ears), then they will have a definite gift and an advantage for musical achievements. If they have a gift for writing, known as rhetoric, and also a high score on Imagination, they will have a trait cluster which would be the ideal traits of a composer or songwriter. If they also have good hand dexterity, playing a musical instrument will come naturally to them. If no lines are visible, this should not discourage anyone from wanting to sing – it's just that people with this gift do find they have a natural ability, while others may have to work that bit harder to attain the success. Others may find that they just do not have the ability at all, in which case they should not feel discouraged either, as they will have other gifts waiting to be cultivated.

(See sections under Rhetoric and Imagination)

PERSONAL NOTES

PERSONAL NOTES

PERSONAL NOTES

PERSONAL NOTES

AREA TWO: AUTOMATIC TRAITS

MENTALLY OR PHYSICALLY MOTIVATED, RESTLESS

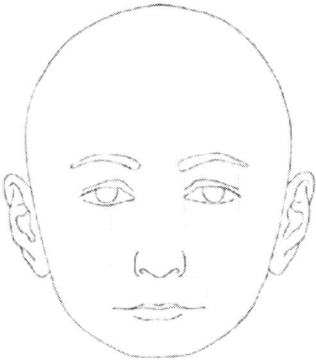
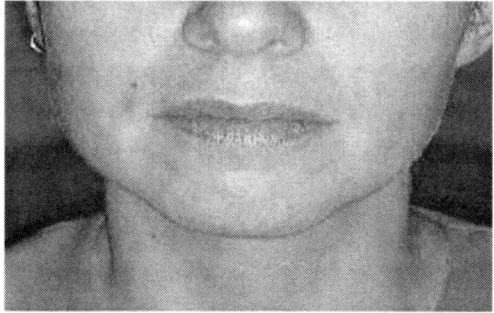

Fig A

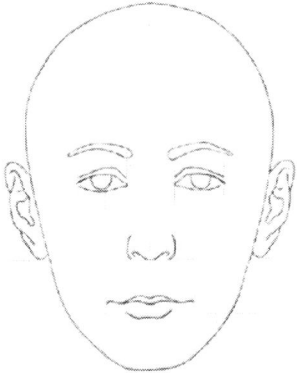
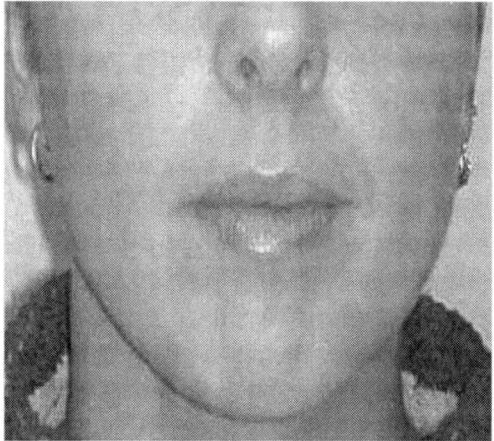

Fig B

Fig A
Example of mentally motivated – the shorter space from nose to jaw of the chin.

Fig B
Physically motivated indicated by the long space from the nose to the jaw of the chin.

MENTALLY MOTIVATED

This trait is found in the "Automatic Trait Area", which is an indication how the person will automatically respond to situations. A shorter lower face is a sign of being more mentally motivated than physically driven, as seen in Fig A. Mentally motivated people tend to think before taking any action. They may appear to be slow at times to become motivated, only making a move after calculating the cost and weighing everything up. At times they may require a push to get them into action as they will sit thinking about it, while others are asking "Why don't they do something?"

An example of this is where an individual is asked for a chair. The first thing mentally motivated people do is stop and think "Where can I get one?" Only when they have thought about it will they move into action. Every situation in life will tend to follow this rule with mentally motivated people. They think first, sometimes at great length, sometimes to the irritation of others who may be waiting for a decision, then they decide to do something about it…eventually! Having said this, in business and professions, mentally motivated people do inspire confidence in others who know that decisions made by them are usually well thought out and everything has been carefully considered. These people like mental challenges and things that stimulate the mind, but just like any physical activity they need to remember to have a break. If they have longer legs, they will tend to spend hours reading books, newspapers, magazines, working on PCs, and basically living everything out in their head.

Weighing up everything and carefully counting the cost is both wise and practical. Such approach to all of life's situations can save a lot of heartache and problems being reaped from bad judgement later on. The decisions made will be more often the correct one due to consideration of all the data and facts. Not rushing into things is a prudent step to follow, especially in financial and relationship situations. Mentally motivated people have to realise others may be waiting for their decision. Continually putting off making a decision, due to always feeling you have got to think about it further, can exasperate your partner and others. If things have to be thought through, then it is good idea to set a deadline and try to stick to it. Often it's found that the first decision you feel and think is the right one. By contrast let's look at:

PHYSICALLY MOTIVATED

A longer, lower face is what identifies this trait in the "Automatic Trait Area", shown in Fig B. Again, this will tell you how people will automatically respond in most situations and any given circumstance. Being physically motivated and very restless, they will hate being tied to a desk job and will need to move around frequently. If they have short legs they will find it extremely hard to relax and sit down. They will tend to react physically without thinking – "act now, think later" is their motto! They will leap into action, not even knowing what direction to take. They just feel they've got to do something about it. They are quick to respond to situations and help. If you were to ask these individuals for a chair, they will be up and looking around for one immediately, not even knowing where they are going.

This is one of the main traits which when out of control, can get people into the most trouble, especially in men who may react with physical violence in confrontational situations. If they have a high score on "Impulsiveness, low tolerance" and even "risk taking", they can be a time bomb waiting to go off. Couples with conflicting traits in this area do well to consider making commitment to a long-term, serious relationship, as this can be the cause of many heated arguments when one partner will always takes prompt physical action and the other partner will always want to stop and think about everything. One thinks the other is too impulsive and never thinks about situations, while the other will become irritated waiting for their partner to make up their mind. Understanding the trait and being reasonable can help avoid undue misunderstandings and bad feelings toward each other.

Being swift to take action, particularly in crisis situations, is a great gift. Fast, prompt action has saved many lives when help was needed and someone quickly responded to the situation, even if they were not sure what to do. We all appreciate the person who knows what to do and gets right on and does it. Physically motivated people get things moving fast and if there is a deadline they tend to stay on top. Sometimes they jump into action without thinking it through and if they are also impulsive they can succumb to making errors and making bad or poor judgement in decisions, some even serious. They tend to make decisions based on experience rather than looking at all the facts. This may be crucial to the outcome. It is vital that one thinks of the consequences before jumping into a situation. Again, like all traits, they are only a problem when out of control. Being reasonable is a key to avoiding conflicts and remembering not to do things too hastily that you may later deeply regret.

Employers might want to consider these traits with employees. For example, having a good, selected team of gifted, mentally motivated people dealing with all the decision-making and planning will result in well thought out constructive plans, being put into action by a team of physically and active, motivated, competitive, forceful, driven people to carry them out. This is where understanding the traits of those around you can bring the best out in them, making everything you do positive and productive. Likewise in marketing, for example, naturally impulsive, verbose people will do all your publicity and advertising as they can't stop talking and will talk to everyone they meet! More on this later.

ADVENTUROUS

Fig A

Fig B

Fig C

Adventurous – high, protruding cheek bones.

High, protruding cheek bones is the trait called "Adventurous". People who have this trait (Fig A, B and C) like to try new things and welcome new challenges. They love to travel and move around: they hate being in the same place too long. Examination of American Indians shows this trait to be very prominent and also among races who like to roam and explore. It is also found among nomads who roamed the plains of Mongolia and China, as well as roaming gypsies. These people tend to get very restless when staying in one place too long or at home. Whereas some would feel it to stressful to keep on the move, in those with a high score on the trait "Adventurous", it's normal and something they just have to do. They become dissatisfied with life if they cannot move on or move around.

Couples with one partner having this trait must show consideration and be reasonable in dealing with their mate, making sure life stays interesting and that an occasional weekend away is all that's needed to satisfy the desire for a little adventure.

Careers where there is a bit of adventure, travelling to new places and taking on new projects, where each day brings a new challenge, are ideal for these people. Having said this, a family head may need to consider the turmoil he puts his family through if he wants to up and move every time his family starts to feel settled. Such upheaval can put enormous stress on family members and there may be a need to consider others and learn to be more settled to bring the trait into perspective and balance. Some people need to get out more, some need to learn to be more stable and settled. Whatever the situation is, controlling the trait and not letting the trait control the individual is the secret.

IMPETUOUS OR IMPULSIVE

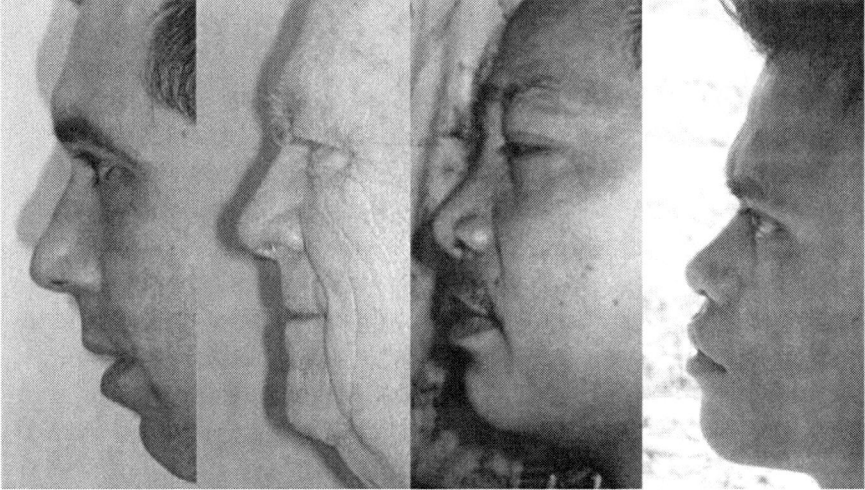

| Fig A | Fig B | Fig C | Fig D |

Low impulsiveness to...   ...high impulsiveness
Receding or protruding lips, mouth and chin. (side profile)

If you can imagine a vertical line drawn between the bridge of the nose and the lips this will indicate whether the person is impetuous or impulsive. If the mouth is behind the line, as shown on Fig A, these types of people will not be impulsive. They will need a really big push to get them going, as they can be negative in approaching things.

Fig B reveals that this individual is still very low on impulsiveness and will not rush into anything. Again he will probably need a bit of a push to get started. These types of people will tend to be reluctant to take up any challenge. As the mouth starts to come forward (seen in Fig C), the more impulsive the person will be in both reacting to situations and making decisions. They will open their mouths before thinking and jump in without thinking. If this trait is out of control, they can get into many difficult situations, much to their regret.

Fig D shows the trait scored as a very high impulsive or impetuous individual. If this trait is combined with risk-taking and high tolerance traits, you can have a real problem on your hands if it is not curbed or kept in check. People who are impulsive will tend to open their mouth before thinking. If they drink, they can be a real embarrassment at any gathering! Impulsive people will spend money on things they don't really need, suffering from what is called "impulse" buying.

On a positive note, impulsive individuals can be very good in marketing as they will very quickly tell everyone whatever it is they are selling and they make good promotions personnel. However, they need to exercise caution about what they jump into, stopping to ask themselves "is this the best step to take, so as not to suffer regrets later?"

CHIN AND JAW

AUTO-RESISTANCE OR STUBBORNESS, PUGNACITY / TENACITY

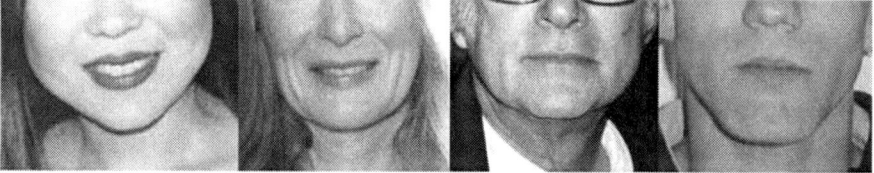

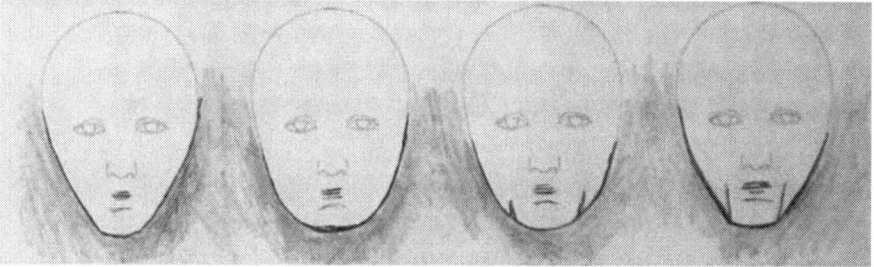

| Stubborn | Non stubborn | Pugnacity | Boxer chin |
| Fig A | Fig B | Fig C | Fig D |

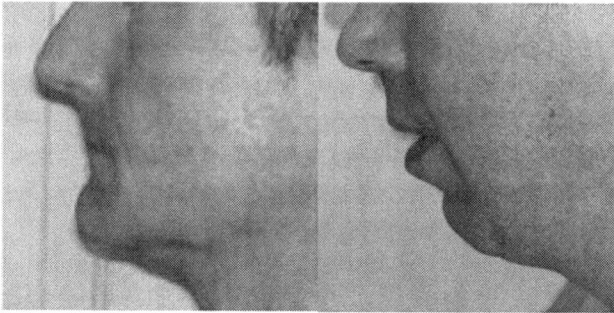

| Fig E | Fig F |
| High tenacity | Low tenacity |

To refresh again, the area from the nose to the chin is called the "automatic trait area" as this will tell you automatically how people will react to situations. The sharp or pointed chin as seen in Fig A is a sign that when told what to do, people with this trait will automatically resist or be stubborn. To get the best response from this type of person, they need to be asked rather than told; they need persuasion to encourage cooperation, such as "I know you're really good at this; do you think you could do this little thing for me?" They will then feel more inclined to say "yes" and willingly do it. If you just tell them, you will see the reaction of digging their heels in! If they have exposed eyelids they will tend to react more rather than thinking with the attitude "Don't tell me what to do". So the best thing is don't tell them but kindly ask them, using tactful persuasion to get a better result and more cooperation.

People with the wider and rounder chin, seen in Fig B, are far more responsive to a request and less stubborn by nature. They also tend to be more easygoing by nature. People who have an oval chin (Fig B) and the top of head the same shape, make great chefs and are usually excellent cooks. The wider, square-looking chin, as seen in Fig C and D, tells us that the individual is pugnacious and will fight for an issue or cause and has ability to be a good mental debater. With regards to being a mental debater, you can see this trait often with lawyers and people in arbitration and diplomatic roles. Many successful women seen in business have this trait, as they also tend to fight and push to be successful.

Pugnacity displayed by a square chin is often seen in those involved in physical fighting, such as in the boxing profession (Fig D). Combined with stubbornness, or as we call it, "Auto Resistance", this makes an aggressive and forceful opponent.

TENACITY

Tenacity is indicated by a protruding chin, seen in Fig E. The more the chin appears to stick out, the more tenacious the person will tend to be and force an issue or not let go of one. These people will push and push an issue, persevere and hang on fighting to get something done. They don't give up easily and they don't like to back down in a confrontation.

The opposite people, as seen in Fig F, are inclined to back down when confronted with issues. There is a tendency to lack self-control or difficulty coping with restraint. People with this trait, who also have traits such as high lust, high sex-drive, low tolerance and impulsiveness, will find self-control quite challenging. They will tend to give into the cravings rather than endeavour to control them. Low tenacity is seen as a sign that the person will avoid all confrontation if possible and will want to avoid conflicts as they prefer to solve things in a peaceful manner, not by force resulting in confrontation.

The meaning of tenacious means to hold fast and not let go, so when this trait is out of control, it is found in those who cannot let go of an issue, who can't let go of a situation and walk away. Even when no more is to be said and it's best forgotten, they want to push the issue into further confrontation. If this trait is combined with physical motive, it may result in erupting into a fight, when in fact it could have been easily avoided. On the other extreme, you will have those who will never stand up for anything and let everything go, willingly letting everybody just walk all over them, almost to the point of being cowardly. If this is your trait and problem, then you need to stand up for yourself and hold your ground.

MOUTH AND LIPS
SENSITIVITY, HUMOUR, VERBOSE /CONCISE
GENEROSITY

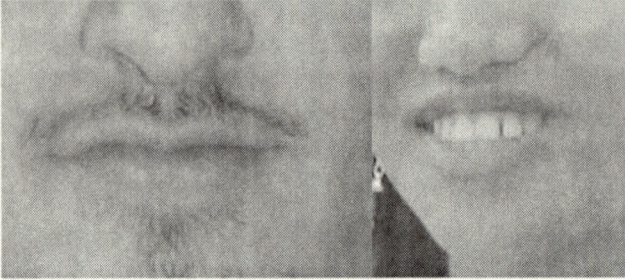

Fig A   Fig B

Above: Examples of high sensitivity

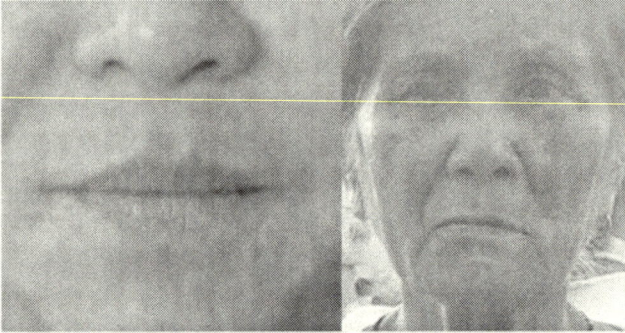

Fig C   Fig D

Likes to talk, enjoys   Dry sense of humour
good conversation   will use selective words

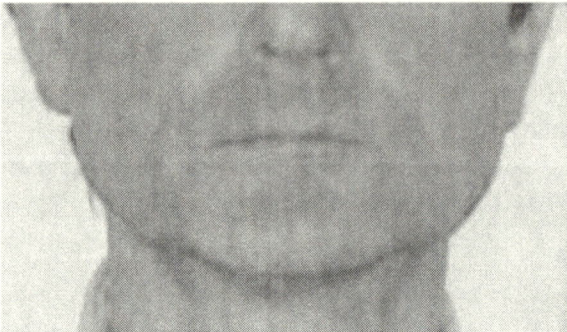

Fig E

More concise, chooses words, talks less

56

The "philtrum" ,which is the space from the bottom of the nose to the top lip, tells us how sensitive a person is and how they will react to situations and upsets. A short philtrum space, seen in Fig A and B, is a sign these individuals are very sensitive and take things very personally. They are sometimes over-sensitive with their feelings. If you upset them, they will brood on it for days and you never hear the end of it. At times, they need to be constantly reassured, as they are very self-conscious and very insecure. They will keep looking in the mirror, checking their appearance and tending to feel they need to keep combing their hair, adjusting make-up and the like.

The interesting thing about this trait is that it's a sign of a very creative personality and women, particularly, are great shoppers and will tend to show a great taste in clothes and whatever they purchase. They seem to have a natural ability and good taste in fashion and like looking good, which explains why they're always checking the mirror. People with a short philtrum space always seem to have a great sense of humour and are good fun to be with. Indian and Pakistani women have a very high score with this trait.

A long philtrum (Fig C and D) is associated with those with a really dry sense of humour, more prone to be sarcastic and is often associated with poor dress sense. The longer the space, the worse dress sense they appear to have and are not really interested in their appearance. They can also come across as being a little more serious. The width of the philtrum is also of interest. The wider the philtrum space, the less concerned they are with words. They will speak very bluntly and openly, whereas the more narrow the width of the philtrum, the more cautious and discreet with words they will tend to be.

The thick upper lip (Fig C) indicates a trait called "verbose". These people like to talk; they enjoy conversation and will tend to talk whenever they get the opportunity. When they answer, they will tend to give you a full reply and sometimes a lengthy explanation and answer. They are also more lustful in nature and imaginative, especially when the trait is found in women. People with thin upper lips (Fig E) are more concise and will talk with deliberate, short sentences, will give straight, direct answers and get to the point. You sometimes feel you have to drag words out of them to get a conversation going. It can be hard work having a one-way conversation when they don't feel the need to express more then the occasional "Yes", "No", "Right" and "OK".

A thick lower lip (Fig C) shows a very generous person who will automatically give for whatever reason. They always give without cause and their instinctive manner is to be a good giver and they are usually very generous by nature. The thicker the lip the more generous they will be. The opposite to this is the individual with a thin bottom lip who doesn't want to give unless there is a real good reason and it is a necessity. They will come across as being rather stingy, mean and sometimes very tight-fisted, especially when it comes to handling money.

Additionally, the lips tell us a lot about the person. The bigger the top lip, the more imagination the person will have and be more lustful. The bigger the bottom lip, the more generous they will be and the more physically driven. Here we see some other interesting things. Some people have a bigger top lip and thinner bottom lip. Here you will see a situation where they have great imagination but little physical stamina to carry it through. Contrary to this is the thin upper lip and bigger or thicker lower lip, sometimes found in men who are very physical and may like to brag, "they are going to do everything", but has limited imagination to actually carry it out.

If the bottom lip protrudes beyond the top, people will be more inclined to get involved with physical acts of violence and prone to welcome a fight. A forward bottom lip and jaw can also be associated with arrogance and aggressiveness, often seen in many offenders caught up in violence and fights. Persons with extreme scores in these traits need to exercise control, be balanced and not let the trait control them. Knowing how to identify the trait and examine our own traits, we can understand why we may feel drawn toward some activities or situations that could reap undesirable consequences and thus avoid them.

AUTHORITATIVE

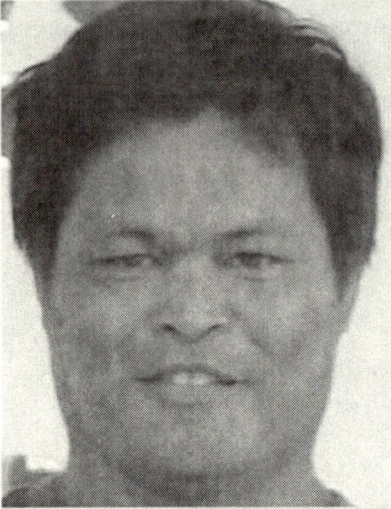

Fig A High Authoritive

Fig B Low Authoritive

People with a wide face and jaw-line always come across as more authoritative (see Fig A). Some people have extremes in this trait so that they appear to have a face that looks like an upside down bucket. These people will tend to automatically take charge. They come across as very self-confident and sometimes rather annoying to narrow-faced people as they like to feel they are the boss and naturally assume they are in control. Wide-faced people should show consideration towards narrow-faced people as they can be intimidating and somewhat over-powering in authority. This does not mean that they are more qualified or suited for the position. It is, for example, like an adult with a loud voice standing over a small, sensitive child. The adult might be very friendly and smiling, but the over-powering effect can often cause unease and feel threatening. So, when some wide-faced people walk into the room with a rather over powering attitude and voice, they can, in fact, make others feel a little uncomfortable. In the right place, of course with the right attitude, wide-faced people are good in positions of authority as they can gain the respect just by their presence. Again, it's using what we have to the best of others' interests, never taking advantage of a situation just because we may look the part. People should respect us for who we really are, not for appearance's sake.

A narrow jaw, compared to the width of the face is less authoritative (Fig B). They may find at times they are not taken seriously. People in professional positions, especially women may find it to their advantage to wear black or dark colours when choosing suits to reinforce their air of authority when having to stand before others in presentations, lectures, or in any legal or political role. Posture also adds to the authority of the person. If a person stands with round shoulders, and not upright, he will lose authority even if he has a wide jaw, whereas a person who may appear less authoritative in the face can come across as having good authority, simply by standing erect, having good posture and paying attention to his or her presentation by being suitable dressed and well-groomed.

SELF-RELIANT

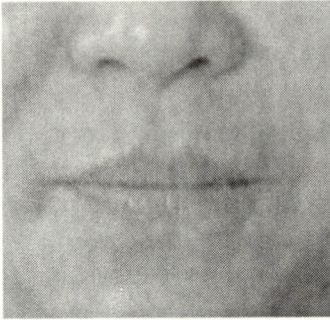

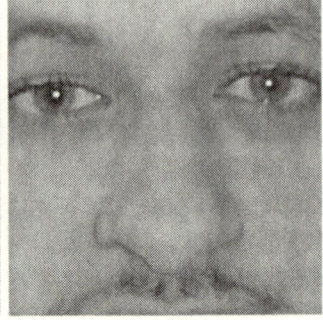

Fig A	Fig B	Fig C
High self reliant	Low self reliant	More physical aggressive

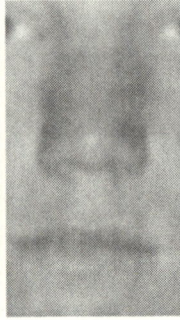

Wide, flared nostrils (Fig A) is a sign that a person is very self-reliant and confident. These people like to stand on their own two feet, whereas those with the appearance of pinched nostrils (Fig B) tend not to be as confident or self-reliant. People with pinched nostrils (like Fig B) tend to rely on others to tell them what to do and need constant assistance and direction, being hesitant to do things on their own. They tend to always want approval for whatever they do. Self-reliant people will take up the challenge, going it alone if need be. They just feel they've got to do it, as others will not do it properly. They have a tendency to want to take over and run the show as they lack confidence in anyone else doing it. The more flare of the nostril, the more self-reliant and independent the person will tend to be. Some people are so self-reliant, with an attitude of "I'm in charge here", that they appear to have nostrils like a snarling bull when you look at them.

The end of the nose shows an inquisitiveness about news and information; hence the expression "nose for news" Those with a bulb-like nose in appearance (Fig A), like a ball on the end of the nose, like all the general news, chat and talk about everything. Those with a sharp or pointed nose (Fig B) tend to be picky and prefer all the gory details. For those who do research, for example, checking the nose reveals the sharper the nose and more pointed it is, the more they will dig deep for every detail until they unearth it.

In men, a really large bulb-end nose can also be a sign of violent tendencies. The swollen-look over the bridge of the nose, as in Fig. C, is also a sign of aggression and possible violent tendencies if not kept under control. It is also referred to as the boxer's nose. If they are physically motivated and impulsive, they can lash out without warning, often getting themselves in trouble due to fights that could have been avoided. If they are very sensitive, with a short philtrum, they will be a person who will lash out and punch someone and then be extremely sorry…until the next time. If repeated, each time they will be heart brokenly sorry. If a woman has a partner like this, she will have to think very seriously to decide how many times she is willing to take a beating or slapping and be forgiving! Not all men with this trait are aggressive or violent, by no means. Many men have this trait yet don't let the aggression surface, but it's wise to be cautious, when contemplating a long-term commitment to a relationship, look at the man's general behaviour and how he deals with others before saying "I DO".

We might, at this point, mention that the cultivation of the inner person is important for good moral character and principles. It will be a big step forward in bringing traits under control and directing them into a positive direction. It's regrettable that today so much is said about our outer appearance and getting rid of those wrinkles, as if this is the be-all-and-end all to happiness. It is not.

Success and the path to true happiness is not a smooth face without wrinkles, but a well-balanced temperament and being able to have self-satisfaction that you are bringing the very best out of yourself and using your full potential with whatever gifts you have inherited. When you have contentment and purpose in whatever you are doing, the odd wrinkle will not be a worrying issue! I see many women who are very beautiful and men who are handsome, but behind the mask they lack joy and inner happiness because they have failed to cultivate their characters and have let their dominant traits control them – the "me first" attitude, selfishness, inconsiderateness, impatience, being domineering and discriminating, having little sympathy for others, impulsiveness, thoughtless risk taking and such like, all having a negative impact on their lives.

TACTFULNESS VERSUS DIRECTNESS

Fig A Tactfulness

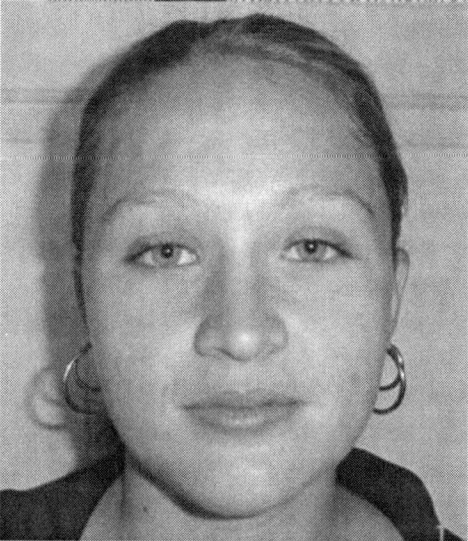

Fig B Directness

Tactfulness is shown by the indent on the side of head at the end of eyebrow (Fig A) People who have this trait will come across as very tactful, will choose and use words carefully and be thoughtful and very diplomatic in approaching situations. This trait looks like as if there is a sharp corner to the side of the forehead and in some people the indentation is quite prominent on the side of the temple area of the head – in extreme cases it can appear as a slightly hollow area. This is often found in lawyers, doctors, arbitrators and diplomats. They just seem to have the ability to say the right words and are careful never to offend but will win a person over with carefully chosen words and phrases. They can present what might be called a delicate topic or confront you with information without embarrassment to themselves or others. They are people of utmost discretion. People having this trait need to be aware that they can sometimes come across as a little infuriating to others because of not saying exactly what they think or should say.

This was, in fact, the very first trait that Judge Edward V Jones noticed while presiding in court. Some lawyers were so tactful that they came across as if wanting to hide something, while others were brash, bold and somewhat intimidating. It was this trait that caused Judge Jones to start to investigate the mug-shots of criminals and offenders who came before him, examining facial traits over the next 20 years of his career as a judge. He became such an expert at studying faces of offenders, he could predict their crime as soon as they entered the court. On one occasion, Judge Jones demonstrated his ability as a personologist and picked out a well-known thief from 500 people at a New York police station. He did this by concentrating on the person who's traits would be the most likely to have committed the crime if out of control. His accuracy amazed the police department, who then took him seriously and with whom he gained great respect.

DIRECTNESS

Directness, on the other hand, is seen by the round, full smooth head with no side indentation (Fig B). These people are very direct, saying exactly what they think even if it hurts. They can come across as very offensive or rude, completely tactless and sometimes very hurtful to the recipient. They tend to lose friends easily as sensitive people will be inclined to feel hurt as if insulted in their company and want to avoid them. They may, in fact, be quite correct in what they say. They just don't use tact in dealing with others, which can often offend. If they have course hair it will intensify the trait. The positive side to this is that when something needs to be said with no nonsense, they are ideal for the job as they will, as they say, "shoot from the hip". People who are very direct don't think they are offensive and will comment "I'm just being honest", and they are; they just don't seem to have any awareness that what they may say could upset someone or cause them hurt when they are on the receiving end of their sarcastic or blunt remarks.

The Chinese are well known for having this trait. Once observed was a Chinese waiter at a restaurant who was asked by a customer "can I have some more of this please?" The waiter said bluntly: "No, you can't", and walked off. It was observed that every statement he made was done in the same tone and manner, yet he was a very pleasant guy. His head told it all! He just said exactly what he thought, not thinking about the customer's sensitive feelings. The customer was most upset by his remarks and said she would never return. Understanding this trait can prevent hurt and bad feelings if people respond in this manner. They may, in fact, be the nicest of people but they are just very direct. Sensitive people should be aware of this, so as not to be overly sensitive or offended by this cultural trait.

THE NOSE
SCEPTICAL / TRUSTING,
MINISTRATIVE / ADMINISTRATIVE

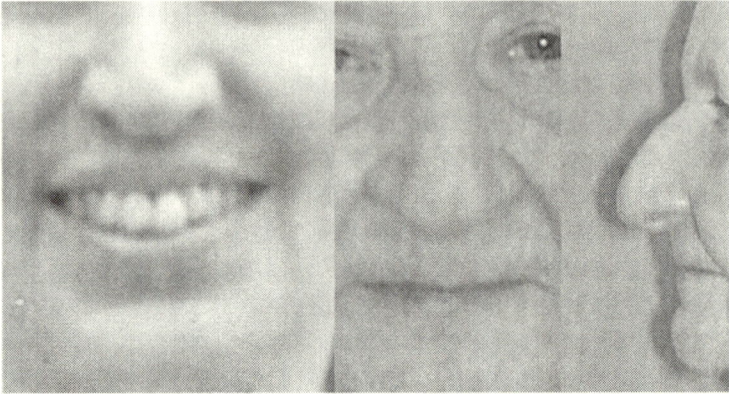

Fig A   Fig B   Fig C

Sceptical and more administrative

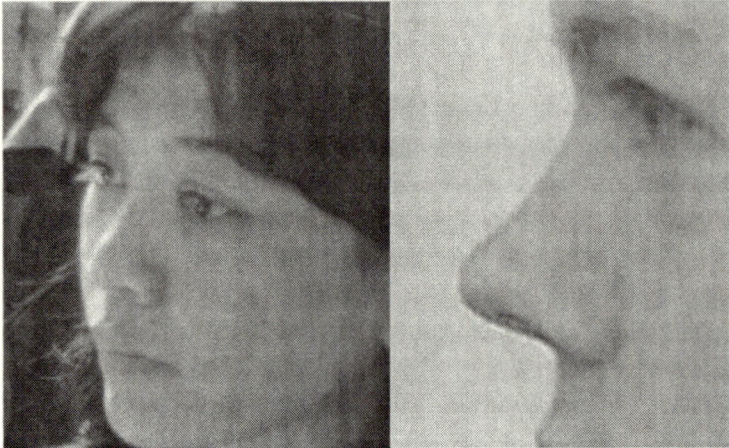

Fig D   Fig E

More trusting, gullible, and more ministrative

The convex nose, or what we might call the Roman nose (Fig A, B and C) is a sign of "administrative ability" and people with this type of trait will tend to take over and run the show. They will automatically feel they can oversee and direct others. They are very price orientated and good bargain hunters; want the best deal and will fight for a bargain and hang onto their money until they get that great deal. Hence the expression "having a nose for money", as seen by many from the eastern culture who own local grocery corner shops.

The "concave or sky jump nose" (Fig D and E in side profile) are "ministrative" by nature and will naturally like to serve and help others. You will see these people working in shops, hospitals and anywhere where they offer a service. If they have ears flat to the head they will spend money very easily and tend to give everything away even to the point of leaving nothing for themselves, as they have an extremely giving nature and to want to help everyone.

Those with a turned up nose (Fig D and E) are very trusting and, in some cases, extremely gullible. Again, if they have ears flattened back, they will be big spenders, money will go through their fingers like water. They really need to learn to be good money managers and budget their finances. As they are very trusting, more gullible and more often fail to question things, they can be taken advantage of easily and a salesman can see them coming! These people really need to question everything, because as they are so trusting, they tend to accept everything often to their later regret. Women, particularly, with this trait need to question things when in a relationship, never accepting things blindly on trust, because many are easily fooled into believing a cunning man due to this trait.

Observation, in the Philippines, for example, found that the up-turned nose was one of the main traits of Filipino people. It's no surprise that religion has such a powerful hold as no one ever questions anything (nor even considering doing so), but accepts blindly what ever they are told. Many a woman has been left holding the baby from being too trusting in relationships. She listens to the sweet-talking promises of some handsome, persuasive man who promises to give her the world, but instead gives her a child with no support and then disappears when its time to take any responsibility.

Opposite to this are Fig A, B and C which show the down-turned nose, often called the witch's nose. These people are "sceptical". They doubt and question almost everything and even if they have all the facts, will reply "I don't believe it". These people also need to be reasonable and trusting when it is required. For a salesman, it can be almost impossible to sell something to a sceptic. When dealing with people who have the trait of being sceptical you need to get all your facts, data and evidence well prepared. If you ever have the need to appear before a judge and he is a sceptic, you'd better make sure your lawyer has thoroughly prepared your case and done his homework, otherwise he won't believe a word of it!

In searching for a sceptical person is was almost impossible to find one in the Philippines, where we were visiting and preparing some of the information for this book. Further examination of university graduation manuals, for example, comparing hundreds of photos, found not one single person who was sceptical. They all displayed the trait of being extremely trusting in nature. If you are a person who has the trait of being very trusting, although it is an excellent quality, we cannot emphasis enough, for your own protection, the need to seriously question things and NEVER take things for granted. Don't accept what might be empty promises, no matter how much in love or moved by emotion you may be.

OPTIMISTIC OR PESSIMISTIC

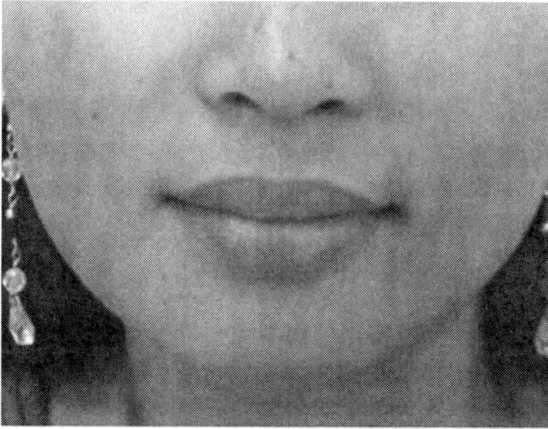

Fig A
Optimistic and positive

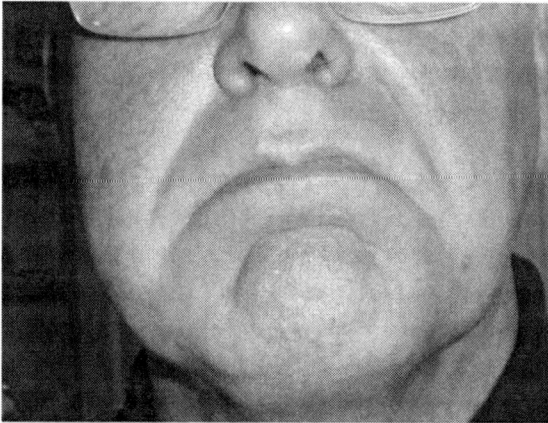

Fig B
Pessimistic and negative

No child is ever born with a down-turned mouth, but one's attitude and thinking in time soon reflects the way a person views things generally and this comes across in the expression of the mouth.

Fig A
To the optimist everything has a positive side and they look for the good and advantage in all situations and opportunities. They appear to be smiling even if they're not, as the mouth will tend to turn upwards.

Fig B
The pessimistic person will see the same opportunities and put a hedge of completely negative thinking around himself. He will totally drain the energy of those associated with them. They tend to monger or peddle fear, putting a block on every opportunity. They only ever see the possible failings or weaknesses and problems of any task. Success is a mind-set and those who are pessimistic need to seriously consider changing their approach to things as well as their attitude. Positive things happen to positive people, negative things always befall negative people.

Two people running a business can be confronted with the same situation. The business is thriving and the optimist sees the great potential and possible good income from being busy, even if they have to work that little bit extra to cope with the demand. The optimist welcomes the success, getting others to help them. The pessimistic person complains that he will never be able to keep up with demands, feels he has got too much on his plate and constantly complains of being over-worked. He disheartens fellow employees by his moaning and negative complaining as he can't see the good, positive result of the income, rather all the additional tax he will have to pay. If he were to earn one million of whatever currency he would only see the one million demands to pay 60% tax. He wouldn't see the opportunities for an extra 40% income, times one million!

PERSONAL NOTES

PERSONAL NOTES

PERSONAL NOTES

PERSONAL NOTES

AREA THREE: ACTION TRAITS

COMPETITIVE, PROGRESSIVE, FORCEFULNESS

Fig A

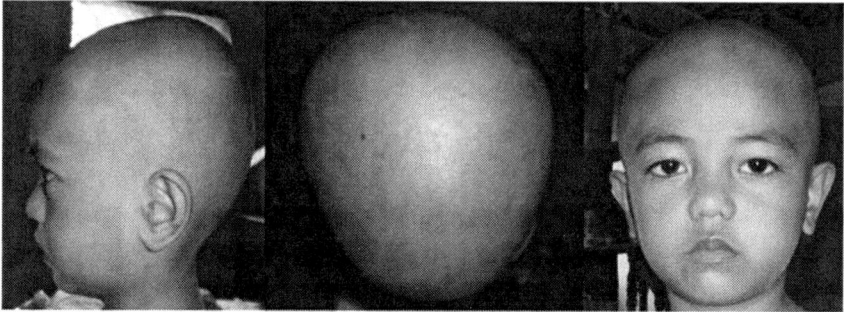

Fig B   Fig C   Fig D

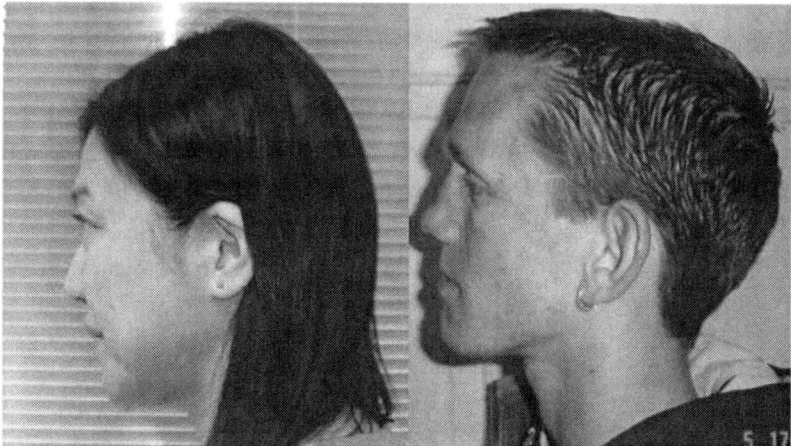

Fig E   Fig F

When the back of the head is narrower in appearance than the front (Fig A) we call this low progressive. It's usually combined with low competitive drive, a feeling of reluctance and tendency to procrastinate. These people tend to dream more than act: everything is "I will do this later or do it tomorrow", all with very good intentions, but "later" never comes. They are often found to be the most kindest of people, with a great willing attitude, but they just don't seem to see or feel any urgency about doing or carrying out anything that may need doing by the time it's required. You can't get angry with them as they are usually the most pleasant of people: they just have a different perception of what "now or today" means!

These people, by nature, are less competitive and will tend to do things just because they really enjoy them, not out of a competitive spirit. They tend to get irritated by those who are competitive as they feel they just want to do things for the fun of it and enjoy it.

The opposite to this is those with the back of head wider than the front, seen in this child in Fig D. They are very progressive, like to move on things, a doer rather than thinker, will tend to have lots of drive, want to get things done, get into the action and win! A person with a head wider just above the ears than front of the head are more competitive, has a strong drive to compete, hates loosing, will feel the need to be the best in everything and always likes to be number one. Sadly, some with this trait do become number one in whatever they pursue, but often lose the real joy they first had in doing whatever it is.

FORCEFULNESS

Forcefulness is seen in the back of head being higher than front (Fig B and E). Forcefulness can come across sometimes as pushy, but these people have a strong drive to accomplish pursuits. They can also come across as headstrong, bossy or as self-willed, but they will get the job done and they make great marketing personnel.

The opposite trait is seen in Fig F where the front of head is higher than back. These people are idealistic and full of ideas but often fail to carry them through. They then get agitated if someone takes their ideas and markets them. They make great inventors – full of ideas and imagination – so if you have a company and want someone to give you lots of ideas, look for one of these guys! Never think your children are too young for you to start to teach, guide and prepare them in a career move. Good planning can pay off if parents observe the gifts in their children.

The example in this section is of a little boy aged five years and who has some amazing traits. He has all the traits of being a potential success in marketing and business and the potential for excessive drive. He has high "progressiveness", high "forcefulness" and extremely high "competitiveness". When we see all three of these traits together we call this a "flying wedge". Parents should look at their children to observe their potential gifts and study their traits. From an early age children can be guided to bring the best out of their traits by cultivating their gifts and giving them good, sound direction in studies and subject matter.

AREA FOUR: FEELINGS AND EMOTIONAL TRAITS

SELF-CONFIDENCE

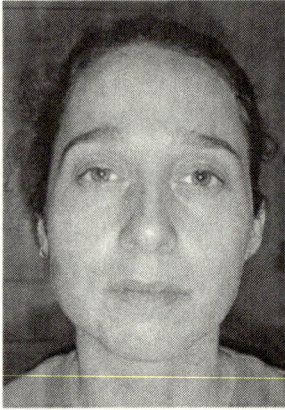
Fig A

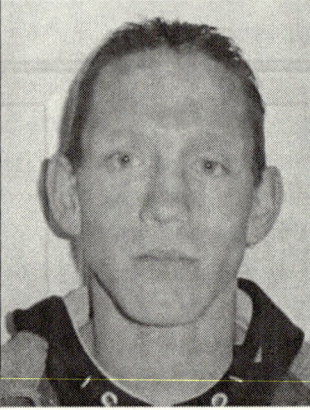
Fig B

Fig C

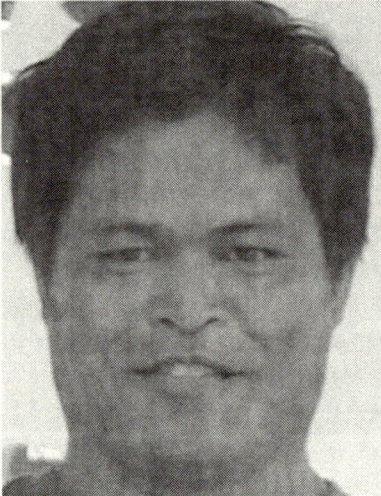
Fig D

Fig E

LOW SELF-CONFIDENCE – slim or narrow face

Examples Fig A, B and C are of narrow faced type people which is associated with less confidence. These illustrate the trait of not being naturally confident. These types of people tend to build confidence through knowledge. Such individuals always want to learn more and are always taking courses as they never feel they have enough knowledge. Even when they have all the qualifications, they still feel a need to keep studying and want to learn more.

At times low self-confidence results in not wanting to take responsibility because of the fear of not being able to handle it. They may feel uneasy about having to think for themselves when they would rather someone else think for them. If this is a problem, the best way is to take small steps and take on responsibility gradually and build confidence. But it should be progressive, allowing you to take on bigger things as time goes by. Think for yourself, plan it all out and then, after you have done this, maybe ask others for feedback. Don't just let everyone else think for you otherwise your progress will be slow.

People with low self-confidence feel no need to travel often and prefer to stay at home rather than move around. The traits show they are less adventurous, as seen in the more shallow check bones. Having said this, they do make great students and will more likely study everything in great depth and are usually very conscientious in approaching projects and academic tasks.

HIGH CONFIDENCE – wide face

Examples Fig D and E are of wide faced people – those associated with high confidence. These examples demonstrate that they will automatically have high self-confidence and will act on limited knowledge. They sometimes feel there's no need to study to get more information. They are more likely to bluff their way through situations for the sake of getting things going than a narrow faced individual will. They tend to take charge and be in control and come across as being more authoritative by nature, as well as very confident. They will come across as having confidence in almost anything they do. They feel they can handle the situation and just take everything in their stride.

For relationships, the width of the face is important to consider, as the more authoritative self-confident person (wider jaw and face) will feel frustrated with the less authoritative, low self-confident person (narrow jaw and face). They will feel the other partner never wants to move on things or is never ready. Vice versa, the lesser will feel the other is too dominating and always pushing them or being demanding. A further situation occurs if the woman is more authoritative. It can, in some cases, intimidate the man, as she will naturally want to be the boss and take control of everything.

On top of this, there is the matter of children born from such a relationship where the widths of the face do not match. The children will have asymmetry and thus suffer mood swings and be temperamental. This can make child-rearing a serious problem rather then a pleasure. The greater the difference in the width of the faces of a couple the more serious the mood swings in the children born from such a union. In some cases the mood swings can be extreme (see section on asymmetry for more information). If there is asymmetry in the face it can affect every other trait in mood swings, either low or in some cases very extreme. As more mixed trait couples join in

82

relationships as well as cultures, the more risk of serious mood swings in the next generation due to both parents being very different. Couples do well to seriously consider this before contemplating having children.

FORWARD AND BACKWARD BALANCE

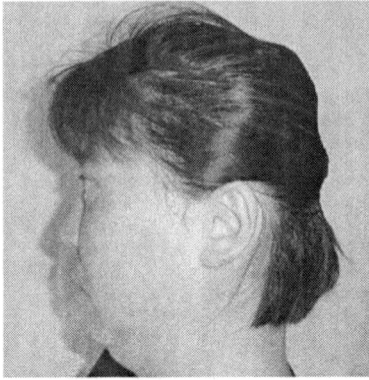

Fig A

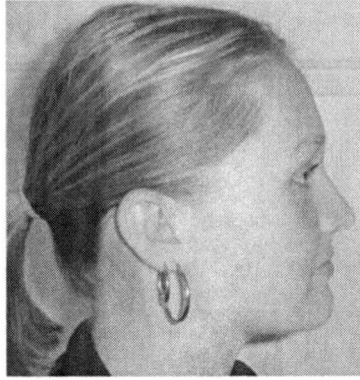

Fig B

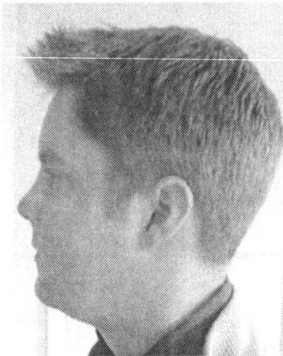

Fig C

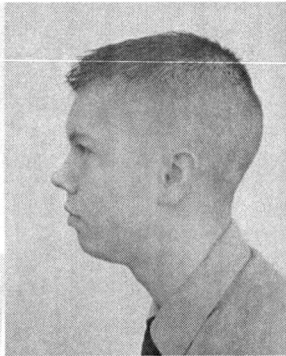

Fig D

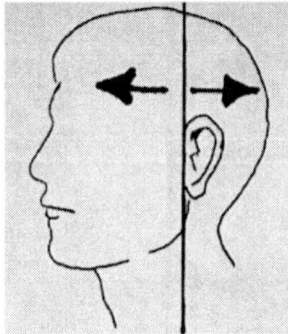

Fig E

The more head in front of the ears rather than behind (Fig A and B) is what we call "Forward balance". These people like to move forward, need lots of recognition and will tend to be out in the front of things. Fig E illustrates the point of measurement. These people are very progressive and not interested in yesterday but more in today and tomorrow. They will not hang onto the past and will want to forget hurtful experiences and quickly move on. Unfortunately, when this trait is out of control, they are prone to tantrums and you will often see this in forward balance children showing off, screaming and stamping their feet. Due to their drive to fulfil their ideals, their attitude can sometimes come across as selfishness, with a "me first" attitude, because the most important thing in their life is themselves and what they want. Everything revolves around them. Having consideration for others can be a problem, as self interest tends to predominate.

On the positive side, if they are in business they will push themselves and get very good results and can be very successful. They just have to remember not to walk over others to get results. These types of individuals seem to know what they want and go out to get it, rather then just thinking about it, which is very positive. When they want a thing they will be happy to go it alone to get it, rather then wait around for others.

The opposite case is when more head is found to be behind the ears than in front (Fig C and D). This is called "Backward balance", These type of people tend to like to work in the background and make great support workers. They have a habit of not letting go of the past and prefer to live there. If they have had any emotional turmoil they will dwell on it for ages and dig up the past in conversation or in arguments, sometimes bringing up the same things over and over again. Another tendency is to daydream.

School teachers can keep an eye on children who have this trait, possibly letting them sit nearer the front of the class to make them focus more and reduce the tendency to daydream. They are by nature more considerate, do not like being the centre of attention, will tend to take interest in history and like old things and the past. If they collect things, it will most likely be older things rather than modern items and memorabilia.

All the young men training in traditional ballroom dancing, for example in the 2007 UK competitions shown on TV, where emphasis was put on being a real gentleman, both in dress and poise, when observed closely they all had a very high score in backward balance. Children with backward balance will tend to be more of a quiet nature, more considerate and gentle in disposition. They will sit quietly and work with little trouble or disturbance from them. If there is a tendency to be introvert, they need to be encouraged to mix freely with their peers.

I have often observed in supermarkets and airports, when seeing families together, that the children of backward balance tend to sit reading, drawing or doing some other quiet activity and will do so for quite a long time. On the other hand, the forward balance children will be running, jumping all over the place, climbing over the chairs, generally showing off and drawing attention to themselves. Next time you see a child showing off, or sitting quietly, look at the head and see how much head is in front of the ear and how much is behind the ear. It's an interesting observation! If you have children of your own and they are all different, check this out between the noisy ones and the quiet ones.

TOLERANCE

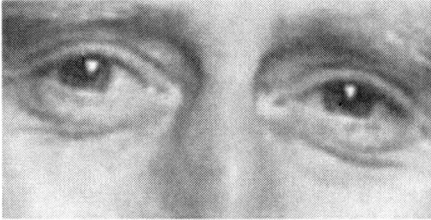

Fig A

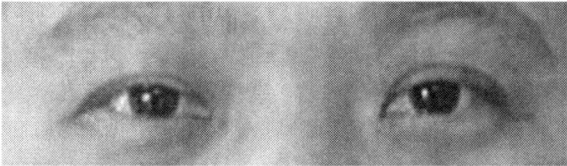

Fig B

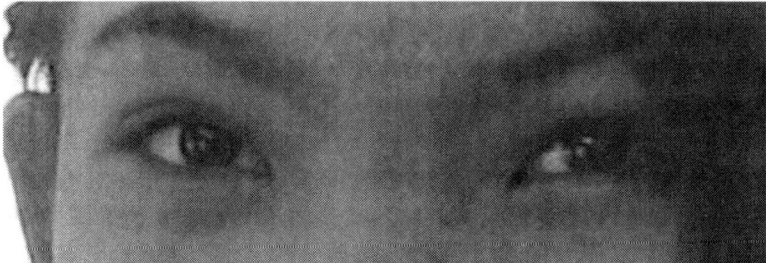

Fig C

LOW TOLERANCE – close-set eyes

Tolerance is measured by how long it takes to upset a person or to get a reaction from them when things irritate or agitate them or when things get on their nerves. This trait is identified by the distance between the eyes, for example in Fig A. The more narrow the distance or close set of the eyes, the lower the tolerance. People with close-set eyes do appear to be able to focus well on things and spot a mistake quicker than a wide-set eyed person.

Low tolerance people are quick to react to situations, will get irritated if they see others failing to take action, especially if combined with the trait of impatience (see section on heads and foreheads). It with amplify the trait and their reaction time to situations will be very short indeed.

If you have this trait, you need to be careful not to get irritated or agitated too easily over small things and focus on your endeavours not everyone else's.

In some people, this trait is so dominant that they are referred to as people who have a very short fuse. If the width of the eye just fits into the space between the eyes, then we call this just tolerant. If the space in narrower than the eye this is low tolerance. If the space is wider than an eye, they are more tolerant.

HIGH TOLERANCE – wide-set eyes

If the width of the eye can fit into the space between the eyes, this person is said to be just tolerant. Asymmetry can be a problem with tolerance, seen in the eye area and there can be serious mood swings. For example, the space between the eyes may be equal to the width of the eye, making a person "just tolerant". But then you may find a situation where the nose is off centre, so that the centre line is in fact "off centre". This is called judgement variation and there will be a mood swing in tolerance. One side of the person will be very tolerant and the other side will have very little tolerance. Having mixed tolerance and being prone to mood swings in tolerance will tend to make them a difficult person to live with.

A person with wide-set eyes (Fig B and C) is extremely tolerant. Having high tolerance, they tend to be more permissive or lenient and will put up with difficult situations, They often fail to see if there is a serious need to take action or if discipline is required. They will tend to let everything go which is why we call it "permissive". If they have low tenacity and also low impulsive traits, they will face many problems and issues if they do not control these traits.

In relationships, couples with conflicting tolerance will come up against issue after issue, as one person will want to take action and the other will object, wanting to leave things as they are. In the case of bringing up children, getting them to do homework, for example, and disciplining them will lead to confrontation after confrontation with each parent. The child may play one parent against the other, always playing up to the lenient parent, if an agreement is not reached between couples.

People who are "high tolerant" need to remember to be punctual with deadlines and appointments and be reliable. They need to focus and not overwhelm themselves with too many tasks or jobs that they can't accomplish because of not being able to keep their minds focused on the job.

It might be good at this point to clarify the proper view of traits. Some may say "Well this is me, or "I am who I am" or make comments "I can't change, this is me". While it's true we're all born with a set of traits we didn't choose, the potential of what we can attain is still down to each individual. Some amazing feats have been achieved by people against all odds, simple because they "WANTED" to and created the drive and desire to fulfil their dreams. It's like a bag of tools and stack of timber: what's made depends not on the tools and wood but what lays within the hands of the carpenter.

THE EYES

MAGNETISM, SERIOUS, JOVIAL, SYMPATHY, EMOTIONAL

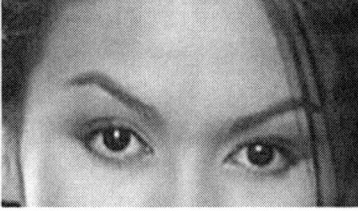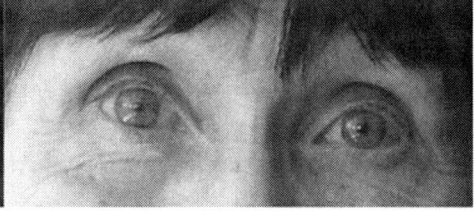

Fig A	Fig B
High magnetism	Low magnetism
rich colour and sparkling	appearance can be dull
very emotional	and little sparkle, less emotional

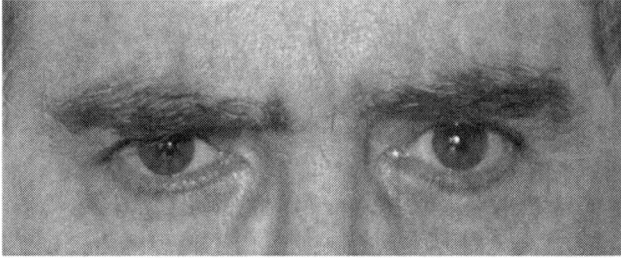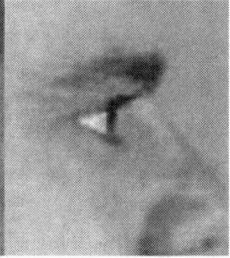

Fig C   Fig D

The overhung brow, deep set eyes, more serious nature

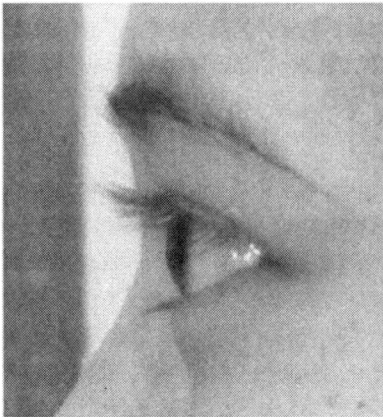

Fig E   Fig F

The protruding eyes, a sign of a more humourous and jovial nature

Have you ever had that experience when someone comes up to you and starts to tell you all their business? They talk to you as if they have known you for many years or as a close friend, then they walk away leaving you wondering why they were telling you all this. It's all to do with "eye magnetism". This is to do with the rich dark iris and sparkle as seen Fig A.
Magnetism is a physical trait but we have included it here, with the emotional traits, seeing as we are discussing the eye area. People, both men and women, but more so women, will often tell you they have had this experience. The more sparkling the eye and rich colour, the more magnetic the personality is likely to be. This may attract undue attention. People will just come up and talk for no apparent reason. If this is a problem with a woman, then a simple solution is to wear a pair of non-prescription plain glass glasses. It does the trick and stops the embarrassment.

One man was very upset and complained his wife was a flirt, as she always drew lots of men around her wherever they went or when they were out socialising. She said she had done anything to draw their attention, but close examination showed she had extreme eye magnetism. When the husband understood this he was better able to deal with the situation. He bought her a nice pair of trendy glasses for going out and it did the trick! Those with high eye magnetism will be more sympathetic and emotional in all situations and have strong feelings and emotions toward others. They need to act on what is RIGHT, not what they FEEL at that moment in time.

People with light or pale colour eyes (Fig B) sometimes come across as cold, yet the opposite may be true and they may be a very warm person. We shouldn't judge people just on the visual appearance of the eye, but it does explain why some get more attention than others. It is also found that people with dark eyes, as in Fig A., are more family-bonded whereas those with pale colour eyes (Fig B), tend to be less bonded to family ties, can be quite independent and go their own way. People with low magnetism, with a small iris, will tend to be less emotional and more unsympathetic toward others. In some cases they can be extremely cold natured.

SERIOUS VERSUS JOVIAL

Deep-set eyes are associated with a serious nature (Fig C and D). Everything in life is a serious business and a big deal to them and sometimes they have little humour. Going shopping, washing the car, anything …it's serious business! They need to view things from the funny side of life once in a while as they can be somewhat depressing to be with, if the trait is out of control. They will become irritated with those who may be flippant, frivolous or have a tendency to joke as they fail to see the humorous side of things. Some people are so depressingly serious and never ever smile. They make you feel you want to go to a funeral to cheer yourself up! On the other hand, they will take responsibility seriously which is a positive side when it comes to commitments. Serious people are more likely to be possessive. Being balanced is the key. Again the trait is only a problem if out of control.

On the other end of the scale are those whose eyes appear to be very forward in the face (Fig E and F). This is a sign of great humour and they will tend to laugh and giggle at everything and see the funny side to all situations. These people also need to realise that there is a time to laugh and a time to be serious. Many West Indian and African races have the trait and you will see women, particularly, with beaming faces and protruding eyes accompanied by a gleaming set of white teeth and huge smile and giggling. Their body never stops moving with excitement over the smallest of things and they laugh as they talk. Everything appears hilarious to them and something to laugh about, responding "sure is honey-pie".

These types of people tend to put life in the atmosphere wherever they go and there is never a dull moment when they are around. Knowing when to be serious and when to laugh again is a matter of simply being balanced and considering the feelings of those around you, so as not to offend, especially when someone is trying to present what they feel is a serious matter. You may want to just see the funny side of it and have a good laugh but this could damage future communications with them if you did.

The signs of crows'-feet, as they are called, on the outside corner of eye are a sign a good humour and laughter and shows a person has a good temperament, as they like to see the funny and sunny side of life. No matter how much make-up or pretence a person may try to hide behind, the eyes never lie. They reveal a wealth of information to those who understand these traits. Lines on the face are seen less in cultures like Japan and China as they tend to hide behind their feelings, never showing them through the face. The face will appear to be solemn and expressionless when they talk. They also hold the body still and never move the hands. Compare this to Italians, Greek and Spanish, whose faces never stop moving and hands never stay still!

In the Middle East they use a system which is called and sounds like the word FA-RA-SA. You will not see anything on the internet and there are no known books written about this subject. But I have a friend who is an expert in this. He simply reads the lines in the forehead and in the area around the eyes, nose and mouth with astonishing accuracy. I'm told they teach this to the woman, who when looking at a man will know everything about him, including how and what he thinks about. You can't lie to a woman or deceive her, if she has this knowledge. She will see right through you even when you say nothing. She will know exactly who you are and your hidden, secret thoughts as the lines will be the result of thought patterns across your forehead. It's an incredible system.

ANALYTICAL, CRITICALNESS, JUDGEMENTAL, UNCONVENTIONAL

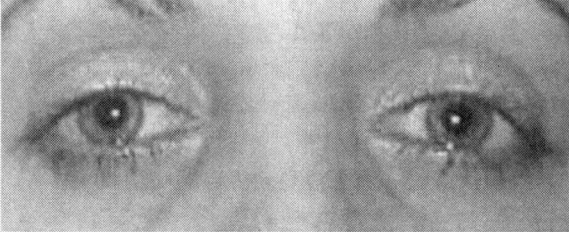 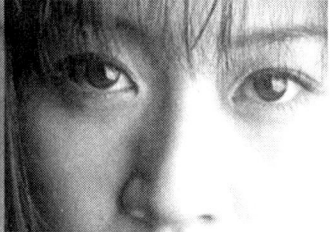

Fig A   Fig B

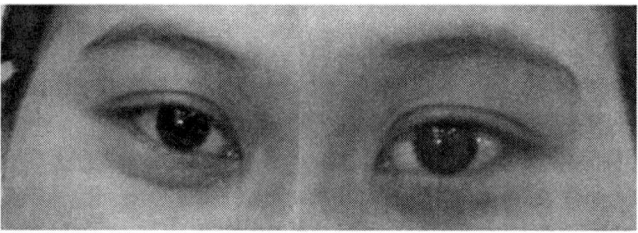

Fig C

Fig D   Fig E

High score unconventional − one eye higher than the other

When the eyelids are exposed (Fig A), we call this low or non analytical. These people are what we call bottom-line people. They like to get to the point and only deal with the very basic facts. They will tend to cut you short or finish off your sentences and interrupt. They get very irritated with lengthy answers so they are great to host meetings as they will cut to the chase and end it promptly. They basically want to know, "what is it, how much, where can I get it?" That's it, any more information and you will see them getting exasperated and agitated. They can sometimes come across as being abrupt. If they also have traits of low tolerance and impatience, this will greatly amplify the trait.

The opposite to this is the "high analytical" individual (Fig B) who likes to know everything, what, why, when, who, how and after all this will still ask you lots of additional questions. They can ask you so many questions that they can wear you out dealing with them. If they also have the trait of "inquisitiveness" they will want to know the complete history before they are satisfied and they will question everything! When western individuals marry oriental partners, they sometimes conflict due to this trait.

One Englishman who had exposed eyelids, as seen in Fig A, would simply say to his partner "do this" or "do that". The man's partner was an Oriental woman with eyes as seen in Fig B. They fought and argued many times over the same thing – he never explained why he asked her to do something. This small thing escalated into big arguments as the female was mentally frustrated, not knowing why she was doing what she was asked to do. When given and explanation of the trait, there was an immediate improvement. From the time they understood the trait, the husband always gave a brief explanation why and if there was no time said: "I will explain later darling", which he did. Knowing that his partner was "high analytical" and how she thought and her feelings, he was able to avoid many stressful situations. She simply wanted to know, why? Even a sentence or two will often be the solution to avoiding relationship confrontations and pointless arguments.

In Fig A, you will notice the eyes drop down or slope downward to the sides of the face. This is called "critical perception" and for good reason. These people will spot every mistake and make excellent employees working with figures. In fact in any profession that has a need for a sharp eye to check quality or data, these people are very good indeed. Unfortunately, this trait is the one that appears to be the cause, because it's out of control, in many marriage break ups. A partner with this trait can be difficult to please and their constant critical approach to things can destroy many a good relationship. If the eyes are close-set it even will amplify the trait to be more critical.

People with this trait will spot, for example, if a picture is not hanging correctly on the wall. They will feel irritated and feel they have just got to get up and straighten it. Everything has got to be just right or it's not acceptable. It's a great trait to ensure quality and accuracy, but needs to be kept under strict control. If not, it can be a nightmare to live with and will ruin a relationship by the person constantly being critical and making the other person feel they will never be able to please. If they have close-set eyes, as mentioned above, which shows low tolerance, you will have a challenge on your hands if you want a very peaceful relationship and quiet life, as they are not very forgiving!

The more the eye shape raises up and outward, as in Fig B, the less critical the person will be and also more forgiving by nature. In fact, you will rarely hear them say a word against anybody. They are also better natured and easier to live with. These people find it hard to spot errors or mistakes. They tend to just see the article or thing without seeing any fault whatsoever. If pointed out to them, they will act as if surprised, and say "I never saw that". If they have wide-set eyes this will amplify the trait and they will have a problem spotting a mistake even if it is big, bold, has flashing bright red lights and right in front of their eyes. A case in point was a woman I witnessed who was working at the bank. She had these exact traits, made five spelling mistakes in one address, but just couldn't see it, even when I stood there pointing out the errors.

BEING JUDGEMENTAL

A word of caution, don't be fooled by looking at this trait without a sharp eye. LOOK CLOSELY. If you see one eye at a higher angle than the other, this is "judgemental" (Fig C) and the person will pick, pick, pick and can drive you crazy fault finding. People with one eye raising higher than the other are also found to be very insecure, need constant reassuring and find it hard to trust others. You will find yourself having to explain every move you make, where you have been and who you talked to and accept being interrogated often if it's your partner.

I spoke to a woman in a Chinese supermarket on one occasion who had this trait – about a 10 out of 10 score! I asked her did she feel she had strong opinions about others or things and she immediately replied "Yes, I know my mind on everything" and then added "I don't trust anybody" and said she couldn't have any relationships as she had no confidence to trust anyone, well, say no more!

This trait is similar to cat's eyes in appearance, but one eye is always at a higher angle then the other. Judgemental people will criticize and pass judgement on everything; they jump to conclusions and can be insecure to the point of being paranoid. They are extremely difficult to live with as you will feel you can't do anything right and can never please them. This trait is seen more in Oriental cultures, particularly the Chinese and Japanese.

A good understanding of people and traits will be of great advantage in preventing people with this trait from being overly-judgemental toward others, if this has been your problem up until now.

UNCONVENTIONAL AND CONVENTIONAL

When an individual appears to always do the complete opposite to everyone else or what is accepted as the norm, they are referred to as "unconventional". People who have this trait can be mild to extreme and it is identified when the inner corners of the eyes are not in line or level, as seen in the mug shots (Fig D and E). It may be only a millimeter or up to seven millimeters difference – but maybe even more. If individuals have this trait, they will tend to do the complete opposite to everyone else. They may come across as disruptive and not following the general flow of things. They are more judgmental, may find it difficult to conform and they hate having to do the same as everyone else. They like to see if they can do things an alternative way. They are, in fact, very creative by nature and come up with amazing ideas and have a flare for creative abilities because they desire to be different. Conventional people, as seen in Fig A, where the corners of the eyes are level, will tend to just go along with the flow and conform with little opposition or problem.

In one situation, where a man found himself in a court of law being accused of an offence, it was argued by the prosecutor that as everyone would normally do a certain thing, then this man must have followed the same path and therefore was automatically guilty. But on examining the man's eyes, he was seen to have a very high score of being "unconventional". The man's explanation was, in fact, very reasonable and his behaviour was in fact typical of an unconventional person who would not have taken what was considered the normal course of action. The finding of this trait and presenting this information to the court saved him from what could have been an unjust sentence.

EMOTIONAL EXPRESSION –
CRUELTY / SENSITIVITY

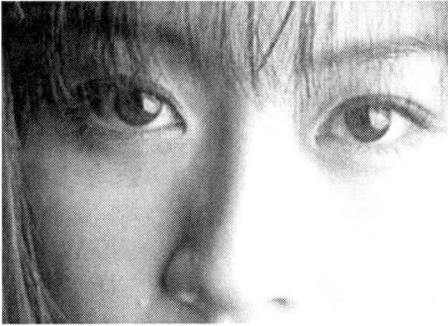

Fig A

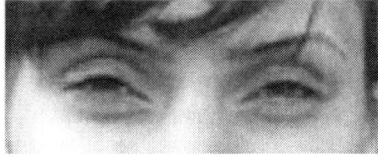

Fig B

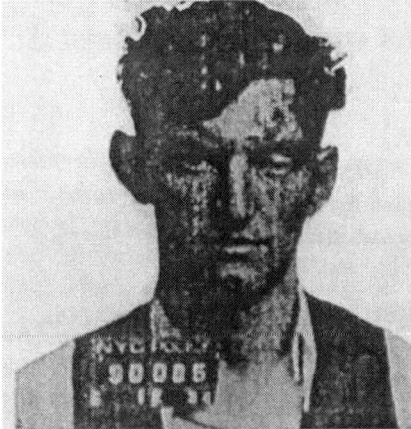

Fig C

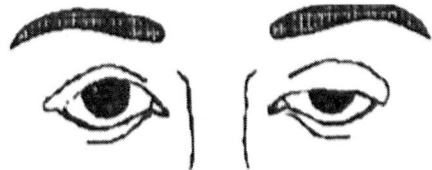

Fig D

Cruelty - one eyelid drops lower over the iris.
Prison mug shot picture contributed by Dr. Paul B. Elsner

Large irises and pupils that sparkle are an indication of high emotional expression (Fig A). The eyes are full of warmth and love; affectionate, kindly and sympathetic. Small irises that look dull tell us that the person lacks emotion, unsympathetic and maybe cold in nature. These people (with large irises) can be very emotional and get involved with others' problems. They need to keep a clear head as they can fall in love easily and also get hurt. They need regular reassurance and comfort. The example in Fig B also tells us that the person is extremely sensitive and will be tearful easily. They almost talk with tears in their eyes and are very affectionate and warm by nature. If they have fine hair it will amplify the trait. This trait is identified by the inner corners of the eyes dropping sharply down towards the nose, making the corners appear longer than average. Those with the trait are exceptionally sensitive and very emotional: they are like a bone china teapot and need to be handled with great care and gentleness.

The "cruelty" trait, illustrated in the mug-shot (Fig C) and illustration Fig D shows that of one eye lid drops down lower than the other, slightly over the iris or pupil. Dr Paul B Elsner found while compiling profiles in San Quinton prison, USA, that every convict who had been involved in murder, assault, violence, cruelty and other forms of physical abuse had this trait, **right down to the last man**. This does not mean they purposely set out to be cruel to anyone, it just means that they have an inner hardness and unsympathetic feelings toward others and that if you upset them they can be really mean and nasty if they choose to be. In some cases they will, in fact, take pleasure hurting others and causing them pain. As we said, there are good traits and traits that can get out of control. You will find these people ideal for working in a slaughterhouse, as butchers, coroners or undertakers, paramedics who deal with gory situations like trying to remove the remains of a suicide from a railway track. These people tend to feel little reaction to situations that would turn another's stomach; to them it is just another routine day's work.

RHETORIC

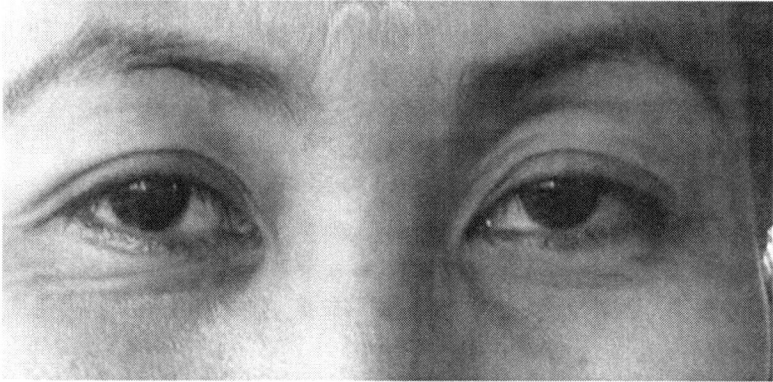

Fig A

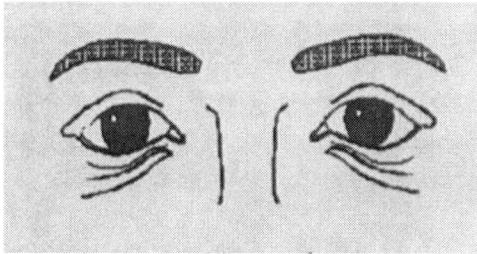

Fig B
Rhetoric - Two lines under the eye

The trait called "rhetoric" is the gift for writing, seen here in Fig A and B. This is where a person has two sharp lateral or horizontal lines under the bottom eyelids running up to the corner of the eyes by the top of the nose. These people just have a natural gift for writing and make excellent editors, journalists, novelists and scriptwriters. If they have the gift of imagination, it will add to their success. If they also have a gift for music, as seen under the ear trait section, you then have a potential musical composer. If two vertical lines are also seen cutting across these rhetoric lines, which looks like $=\#=$ then they also have a gift for languages. A man who loved writing and languages and wanted to learn Chinese also spoke several other languages including Russian. This is something most of us would find very difficult and a real challenge, yet on close examination of this man's eyes, it was very clearly seen he had two rhetoric lines but, even more clear, were the two cross lines under each eye. This man commented that he found both learning, speaking and writing other languages easy for him as he felt he just had the gift for it, and enjoyed it. He was right, he did in fact have a great gift!

It is often found that a person may feel they have a gift and yet parents will totally discourage their children from cultivating it and force them down a path or a career they're really not interested in. This mentally frustrates the individual who goes through life feeling agitated and unhappy, yet doesn't realise it is the gift simply wanting to come out for advancement and to be used. Many a career has been made from what started out as a hobby when the individual found that a hidden talent or skill was sitting there waiting to be cultivated and used. It's amazing that many offenders admit they are mentally frustrated and have no direction, but once given a positive opportunity they can become very successful.

One young offender was told: "You have so much talent, you shouldn't be in this place". On being giving the right advice, he went onto become a successful network marketing businessman and now lives on a luxury yacht and is financially independent. This man didn't have any bad traits, he just had a few out of control and which had been going in the wrong direction, but were now corrected!

THE EARS
ACQUISITIVE, INDECISION, PERSONAL DEVELOPMENT AND STANDARDS

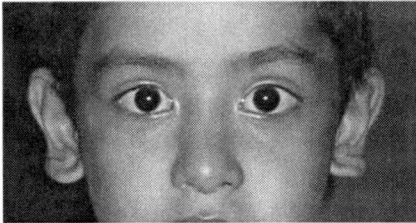
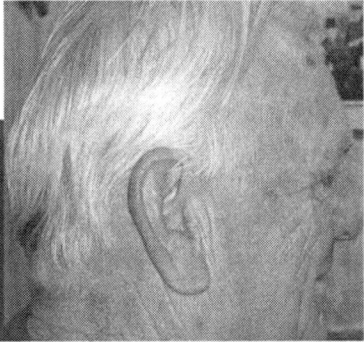

Fig A

Fig B

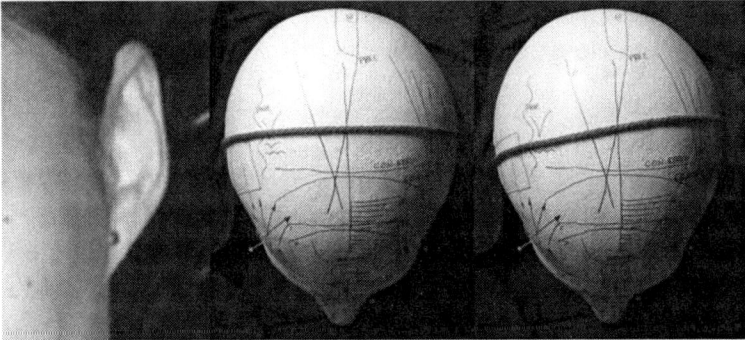

Fig C

Fig D

Fig E

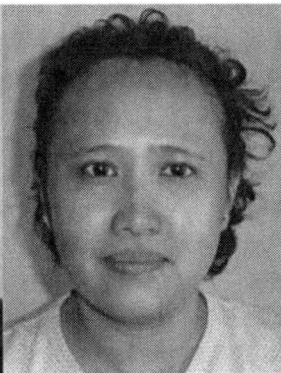

Fig F

Fig G

Fig H

Some people have ears that stick out and they often teased, being called "wing nut" as they resemble wing nuts you secure on a threaded bolt. These people don't seem to miss anything and hear everything that is going on.

This trait is called "acquisitive" (Fig A and H). People with this trait will instinctively ask why and will always want an explanation of how, why, when and so on. Another interesting observation of this trait is that they tend to accumulate and hoard things and surround themselves with clutter but they are usually good money savers. If they have a more Roman or Arab hooked nose, they will make good financial business personnel and bankers, hanging on to their money and fighting for a bargain. If they have flat back ears and an Arab nose, they will have the habit of saving hard and then blowing everything in one go before starting all over gain.

On the point of hoarding clutter, one of my uncles died and I was asked by my father to help clear the house of unwanted clutter. After a few days I couldn't see for such a mountain of stuff that it was unbelievable that it could have come out of one small home. Eventually, we had to get a truck to take it all away. From old engines and car parts to boxes, washing machines, lawn mowers and even a12-foot rowing boat was found hidden outside in the long grass. From clothes to tools, wood, tins of paint, sheets of glass and an endless list of other things, were eventually loaded onto the truck. TWICE! The total load was around 6 tonnes of clutter.

When I studied his photo afterward it was clearly seen why. He had an exceptional high score of acquisitiveness. As with most people with this trait, they just love to collect and hoard things and they really hate throwing anything away. Judge Jones found that the common traits of hoarders and people who steal were "unconventional" (the centre of the inner corners of the eyes were not level) and "acquisitiveness" (protruding wing nut looking ears).

Ears lying flat against the head (Fig F and G) are a sign of low acquisitiveness. People possessing them will ask only the questions that give them the necessary information, and no more. They will have a tendency to spend money easily and can be wasteful. If they have a "ski jump" nose, it will amplify this trait. You may have heard the saying "They saw you coming". The salesman love to see an easy spender. The flat back ears are a sign of this, and if they have a upturned nose as well as flat back ears, then they are very trusting and you can sell them anything as they are easily convinced.

So to all you men, check your wife's ears and nose before you let them loose on a shopping spree with your credit card! You have been warned!

It has also been known that employees who work in business and who have flat back ears and a ski jump nose have a tendency to over-spend. They aren't as price-orientated as those with a convex Arab or Roman nose and out-turned or protruding ears. So if your business is over spending, it might be a good idea to check out who is doing your accounts!

Either extreme has both a positive and negative side. Those with high acquisitiveness are good savers but can also be very mean, not wanting to give anything away even if they have an abundance. They need to learn to give of themselves and time. Likewise, those with low acquisitiveness are very generous and sometimes are so generous that they give away even the things they need and their own possessions. They spend money too easily and need to learn to budget and save.

PERSONAL DEVELOPMENT

Large ears and lobes (Fig B) are common among men, and are associated with individuals who are conscientious about personal development. When found in men they are more inclined toward gardening interests and are more generous by nature. The example in Fig C is typical of people who have little or no interest in personal development and are of a less generous nature. As with all the traits in this book, do not believe what we say, go out and put it to the test! Simply look at other people's traits and ask "do you find you are…blah blah blah or inclined to do…?" The feedback will surprise you. A word of warning: it's never wise to talk to someone and say: "You have this trait so you must be…" as it could offend them if they misunderstand you. Rather it's always best to say: "You have some interesting traits, do you find this…or do you do this". Then add: "People with this trait usually tell me…" and then bring out something positive about the trait, before asking about challenges they may face. Once people open up they will give you lots of information about themselves, and that is great feedback.

If one ear is forward and the other ear back on the sides of head, it shows an indecisive person who has problems keeping to their decisions and is constantly changing their mind. This person will drive you crazy. Fig D shows the line of where ears are balanced, whereas Fig E shows the ears out of line. I knew a woman who was forever changing her mind when shopping, she would pay for the item and by the time she got to the store door, she had changed her mind and took it back to the cashier for a refund….often! Then one day I asked to look at her ears, Wooow! I also met a woman whilst researching who had serious mood swings and problems making decisions. Her ears were about 40mm out of line and her husband was finally relieved to find out why. He said: "she drives me nuts"!

HIGH AND LOW PERSONAL STANDARDS

Likewise one ear higher than the other is indication of a mood swing in standards. They will make an issue one day and let it go the next. Again, this asymmetry is caused by having two parents who are very different. An optician reported that some people return their spectacles complaining that they are crooked and out of line when laid on the table. They are rather surprised to be told: "Sorry sir, it's not your spectacles, it's your head and ears that are out of line".

Ears that look high on the head and in line with nostrils indicate a person who is realistic; they are down to earth and reasonable (Fig G and H). They will view everything with logic and commonsense; will tend to make good, sound decisions and have good judgement as well as having high standards.

Low-set ears on the side of the head, well below the line of the nostrils (Fig F) are an indication of a person leaning toward being far more idealistic. They like to dream and have a tendency to be unrealistic and to ignore sound logic and prefer to live in fantasy world of their own and are prone to make unrealistic decisions. They will see life as it should be and not always as it really is.

MUSIC ABILITY / PIONEER TREND

The rounder the shape of the outer ears, the greater is the gift for music appreciation and a natural gift for music, rhythm and sounds.

Fig L is a good example, found among many professional musicians. This example shows a nice round shape.

Fig K indicates a person who has a good sense for pitch and sound – the outer and the inner ear ridge (called the pinna) form a parallel line shape, often a trait found in individuals working as musical instrument tuners and in recording studios. The thinner the ridge, the higher the pitch people will be more inclined to prefer: the thicker the ridge, the deeper the sounds they find more acceptable within their music tastes.

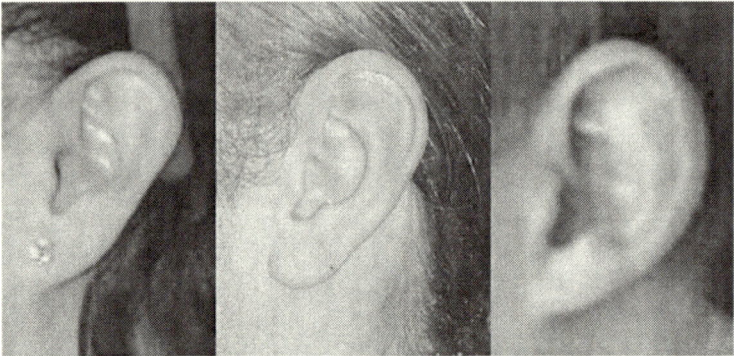

Fig J   Fig K   Fig L

PIONEER TREND

When the outer edge of ear has a straight appearance, it is called the "pioneer trend" (Fig J). These people have a love for adventure and like to work for themselves. They hate working for others and prefer to work for their own business and like a challenge to explore new things. When looking back at old photos, it's been observed that many of those who left their homelands to become pioneers in the New World or life in the USA or the West from the 1860s onward, almost all manifested this trait. It's for this reason that the trait was given this name. They love adventure and new challenges. They like to be their own boss and feel free and not feel hemmed in and tied down, working for someone else.

Those with the "pioneer" trait may, in fact, only have this on one ear in some cases, due to the asymmetry of the face and having two very different parents. One ear may be straight, yet the other ear may be completely round, with no straight edge at all. Most people are not even aware of it, until it's pointed out to them.

The rounder ear shows a more willing attitude to accept being a support or team-worker. The straight edge ear indicates a desire to be very independent and work alone. If an individual has odd matching ears they will have a mood swing in this area; one day desiring and focusing on wanting to be their own boss and another day happy to work for someone else and plod along.

EYEBROWS
DISCRIMINATIVE, DESIGN, MECHANICAL AND AESTHETIC APPRECIATION, PRACTICAL, DRAMATIC.

Fig A   Fig B   Fig C

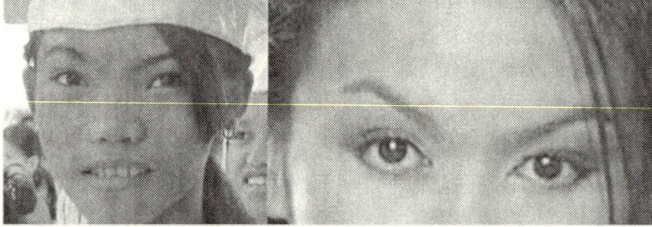

Fig D   Fig E

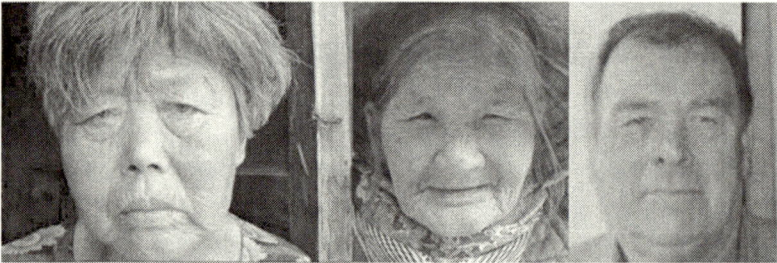

Fig F   Fig G   Fig H

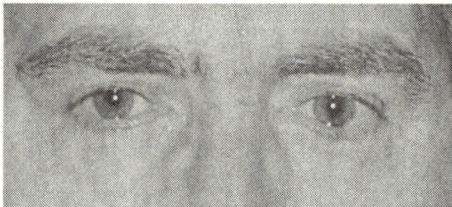

Fig J

DISCRIMINATIVE

High-set, arched eyebrows are seen more in females (Fig A) and indicate a person who likes to keep a little distance and is more discriminating toward others. This person may often appear cold and unfriendly. She may even give the impression and appearance of being unapproachable. The higher the eyebrow, the more discriminate and formal the person will tend to be. This is not to say they are unfriendly, as they may be very friendly but they just like to keep a little distance when dealing with others.

These people will also be more formal in dealing with others. Even having a meal will tend to be a more formal occasion. In fact, almost everything in life will tend to be of a more formal nature. When greeting people who are discriminative, it's good to remember to keep a few feet apart. Hugging and kissing before you really know them will make them feel really uncomfortable. Once friendships are made, they will be inclined to treasure the friendship, but don't rush, push or pressure them into friendship as they will back off immediately. Let them make the first move.

DESIGN APPRECIATION

The shape of the eyebrow in Fig B is known as "Design appreciation". It looks like an upside down "V" or a pyramid on the forehead. These people have an innate knowledge of how things should be constructed. This trait is ideal for persons working as designers, builders and architects. The trait is also found in individuals, such as those who like to build businesses and plan things out. They just appear to know how to structure the project. Young and old alike with this trait will enjoy using creative ability and undertaking projects to put things together.

MECHANICAL APPRECIATION

"Design appreciation" is a gift for understanding how something is designed, while the trait called "mechanical appreciation", seen from the example in Fig C, has eyebrows which look like an upside down half moon and is where the natural ability is being able to bring everything together. These people have the gift for putting things together, such as parts of machinery and furniture. They are great planners and love organization. If they have an oval head (also seen in Fig C), they like working with people and will make good project managers. They have a natural ability to organize functions and events; hence they also make very good events managers. Other interesting things about eyebrows are that the longer they drop down in an arch, as seen in Fig A and B, the more is the ability to organize. Some people have both traits of design and mechanical appreciation, as in Fig B. These people will relish the opportunity of seeing everything undertaken from start to completion.

PRACTICAL SQUARE BLOCK EYEBROW

The longer the eyebrow, the more the desire to build your dreams as the imagination is still strong. In older people, you will notice they develop short, square brows, sitting just on top of the eye, with nothing dropping to the side (Fig F and G). This is an indication that they live a purely practical life and they have no real goals, no dreams and no incentive to do anything. They have an attitude of being pessimistic and have basically given up on life. Their only concern is to survive. They will also appear sad-looking, serious and sometimes look depressed. It is known as the "square block eyebrow".

DRAMATIC

The following trait is called "dramatic" (Fig D and E) and is identified by the sharp angle of the eyebrow from the nose out and upward. Those who posses this trait tend to have a flare for whatever they do. They usually love drama and are found working in theatres and live shows: hence the name "dramatic". They come across as rather flamboyant, sometimes over the top and occasionally eccentric, because nothing is complete unless there's a bit of a drama. They need that big entry! They usually have loads of character, with an artistic creative nature and are fun to be around.

AESTHETIC APPRECIATION

Fig H and J show what is called "aesthetic appreciation". People with this trait need peace and order in life. The identifying sign of this trait is seen in the very straight underside of the eyebrow. These people are very friendly and, as in most traits, it's found in both men and women, although more so in men. They will talk to anyone and come across as very friendly, so if you walk into a room and want to know who to talk to, look for the people with this trait of the low set straight eyebrows. People with this trait like order, and disorder can make them physically ill. They are usually very peace-loving people and it takes time to upset them. However, if they do get upset they totally lose it, exploding and going completely out of control in a bid to get things settled as they like it. Once they have everything under control, they settle very peacefully again. A person who has "aesthetic appreciation" is like a big dog sitting in the yard wagging its tail. He is perfectly harmless until you encroach on his space, upset him or tread on his tail, then his teeth will be swiftly in your ankle! This trait is also very creative and many good craftsmen are seen with this trait. The need to have pleasant, nice surroundings and décor tend to lead to the desire to create nice things, such as painting, sculpture, gardening and so on. I have seen many carpenters with this trait.

PERSONAL NOTES

PERSONAL NOTES

PERSONAL NOTES

PERSONAL NOTES

AREA FIVE: THINKING TRAITS

THE SHAPE AND SLOPE OF THE FOREHEAD

Fig A

Fig B

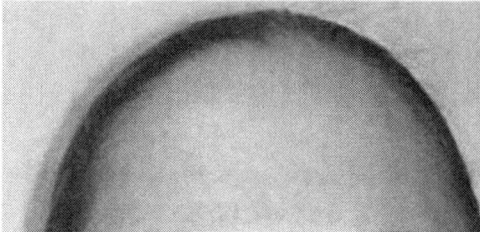

Fig C
Conservationist head type

Fig D
Construction head type

**Which one are you more inclined to be,
are you a potato or brick head?**

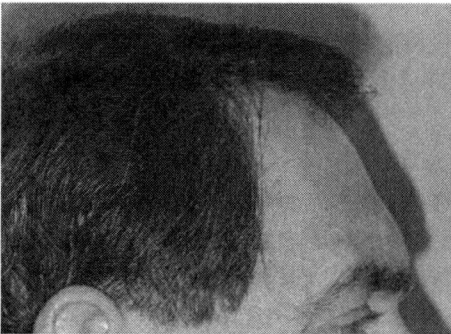

Fig E
Object thinker

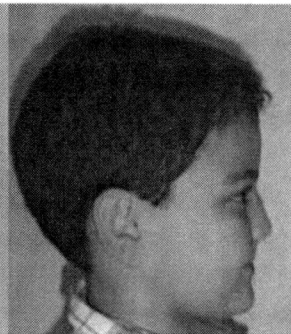

Fig F
Sequential thinker

What has the shape and slope of the forehead got to do with making decisions and carry out maintenance? The following section explains why many couples conflict and argue for no apparent reason. This information is very important if looking for a soul mate.

Fig A and C. The round or oval-shaped forehead is known as a "conservationist head shape", a homemaker who likes to re-use things, is a maintainer, friendly and likes working with people and loves to look after things.

Fig B and D display a square-shape forehead called the "constructionist head shape". The head has square appearance and the person likes a challenge, loves starting new projects, can appear wasteful, likes to start afresh, likes to use new materials, is more career driven and finds maintenance, servicing or looking after things boring.

Looking at the forehead in Fig E, it slopes back (in side profile) and identifies an "object thinker" who has quick reactions, makes quick decisions based on experience, and may come across as impulsive as he spends little time thinking over the issue, but is good in crisis situations. These people make good students and are fast learners.

The flat, vertical forehead, seen in Fig F, indicates "sequential thinkers. They like to learn step-by-step, hate pressure, need time to think and may appear slow. They don't like last minute changes.

Now let's look a little closer at these traits. Doesn't it drive you crazy when you just want a simple "yes" or "no" when people say "well I'll have to think about it". It's a common complaint of many couples where one always seems to know instantly what they want and should do and the other person just feels they have got to leave it and think about it. For example, she says he is impulsive, but he says she can never make any decision until she has a long think about it, and vice versa. People with conflicting traits in the forehead can find they are arguing and fighting for no apparent reason when it comes to making decisions and even purchasing the most simple of items. The simple answer lies in understanding how we process information. Then the arguing ceases to be a problem.

Basically, we only need to look at the slope of the forehead and this will indicate how fast a person can process information and make decisions. This tool is great for people in marketing as that little bit of pressure on a customer could cost you that sale! We'll show you how to deal with this. People with more of a vertical forehead ("sequential thinkers" – Fig F) are step-by-step learners and like everything laid out for them. If they miss a point, they will tend to go back and start all over again. Once they have all the information clearly explained step-by-step, they have excellent recall and the information is always at hand. They like to think everything through and if a decision is made will feel extremely stressed if there is a change of plan. When dealing with sequential thinkers, you need to remember to inform them well in advance of any possible change of plan. If you tell them in advance, they will be prepared and not be so agitated as they would be if you suddenly change your direction. Some children can be teased due to their high flat foreheads, as seen in Fig F.

Sales people, when dealing with a "sequential thinker" type forehead should try to close a deal by suggesting: "Would you like to have 15 minutes, to have a cup of coffee and think about it?" Sequential thinkers will really appreciate this. Giving them just that little bit of extra time and consideration could mean the difference to gaining or losing a sale. If they are still not sure, give them more time. One car salesman who tried this said he never lost a sale, even if the customer came back several times. They really appreciate not having any pressure.

Many children at school have been labelled as slow learners due to this trait, when in fact it has been the teacher's fault not understanding how to pass on information to the pupil. Their minds are like a filing draw with everything in order and they like to put information in order as they learn it, The best way to teach is stage 1, then go to stage 2, and so on. If you throw lots of information at them, they will just shut down mentally and look at you blank-faced! Children can be teased at school, being called brick head or spam head and being asked "is Frankenstein your father?" A sensitive child will find this rather hurtful. Children should be informed of their gifts, encouraged and commended so they will not feel intimidated due to teasing comments from their peers.

"Objective thinkers" (Fig E), with the sloping-back forehead, indicates a fast thinker and quick learner who makes quick decisions based on experience rather than checking all the present facts. They can come across as impulsive and if you get them behind the wheel, it's a fast ride home. If they also have the trait of high-risk taking (see heading "The Hands"), and you get into a car with them, hang on to your breakfast, it will be a white knuckle ride all the way!

"Objective thinkers", by contrast to "sequential thinkers", are quick learners and you can throw them tit-bits of information and it all goes in, although recall is not so good. You can change plans at the very last moment and they will take it all in their stride. They will tend to look at situations and immediately relate this to some past incident and make a decision based on that. As they tend to be a little impulsive, they may have a habit of not thinking before they speak, although they may be correct and make the right decision. They need to remember that getting all the facts is crucial when making more important decisions. "Objective thinkers" are known for their fast reactions and getting things done and are great in crisis situations. It's a common complaint made by many women that their partners just never want do the dishes, or any other domestic chore come to that. But, on close examination of the forehead, we can understand why! These men are not lazy by any means, as they will work very hard in other areas, so what is the problem?

People with round or oval shaped foreheads (Fig A and C) are called "conservationist ". They make very good service engineers and maintenance personnel. They love looking after things and are good homemakers. They never throw anything away and re-use what ever they have, rather than buy new things. The complete opposite is people with the square appearance foreheads who are called constructionist" (Fig B and D). These people hate using old stuff. They like to throw everything out and start afresh. New materials, new projects, tear it down and start again is their motto!

Round head shaped "conservationists" (Fig A and C) are more people-friendly. They love working with people and being around people. Nursing, customer service and general communication careers are ideal for them. Put them to work in front of a machine or in a factory facing a wall and they will tend to be looking around all day for someone to talk to. The home and family are very important to them and, if given the choice, they will choose a home and family over a career. Domestic chores come naturally and they actually enjoy being a homemaker and doing things around the home. They take pride in polishing that treasured little ornament and looking after everything. From child care, customer service, nursing homes to shop assistants, you will see many round "conservationist" type people only too pleased to help you.

Square head shaped "Constructionist" individuals (Fig B and D) on the other hand are friendly and do not have problems when dealing with others, but they prefer to work on things and projects and are happy to spend time working on their own. They are engineers, machine operators, architects and builders. They are more career-minded and not so focused on family ties. They will rip up the garden and lay a new lawn, but don't expect them to mow it when it needs cutting! They will tear down and rip out a kitchen and re-fit a new one but don't ask them to wash the dishes – that's no challenge. They get bored and like new projects and are constantly looking for change and new challenges. They tend to find any type of repetitive servicing jobs or regular maintenance chores just too mundane and lose interest easily. They prefer the next new job as it's a possible challenge or adventure.

These traits can be seen in both men and women. There are "construction square-shaped" headed women who are interested in a careers and there are men who have a "conservationist round head" who love DIY and being a homemaker and who are more than happy to do almost any domestic chore that needs to be done. On one occasion a woman, who now understands her husband's traits, had tried for years to get her husband to do domestic chores, with no result. Now, understanding her husband's view and approach to work, she simply states: "It's time we have a new kitchen". To her surprise her husband replied "You choose it darling, I'll fit it". Knowing how her husband would happily rise to the challenge to tear down and replace things rather than maintain them, she says: "I'm now working on him for a new fitted bedroom, bathroom and new landscape garden".

Most domestic problems are caused simply because we don't understand the thinking process of the other person or how he or she views a project. Once this is solved we can work around these traits and know exactly how to approach them. The woman who thinks her partner is nothing more than a lazy bum, leaving everything to her, may be amazed by some impressive results once she understands how to approach him with a view to getting a job done. Any of you ladies need a new fitted kitchen, bedroom or landscape garden?

IMAGINATION, ORIGINALITY, INTUITION

Fig A Imagination

Fig B Intuition and originality

The trait of imagination is identified by the big, side mounds, high on the forehead, below the hairline (Fig A). Imagination is the gift which generates lots of ideas and people being very creative in whatever field they choose. For those of you who may have been teased about your large bumps on your forehead at school with "You look like Frankenstein's monster" should be glad to know you possess a great gift. The gift of imagination is a wonderful tool. Such people just seem to have an endless supply of great ideas. They will always come up with something new, original and fascinating, much to the envy of those around them who sometimes struggle to come up with a single idea. They appear to naturally think up new ways or ideas in whatever trait cluster of gifts they may have inherited, such as music, writing, sport, art and so on.

Many people seem to think they need a mass of knowledge and study endlessly to reach their goals in a career, yet there are those with a little bit of knowledge but have great imagination and put it to amazing use. A good example of this is that there are very few professors in universities who can say they are financially independent or wealthy, yet they have an abundance of knowledge. The reason is that they impart knowledge, but they don't specialize in how to use or organize it. But a man with imagination who has a great idea can use these men and produce some amazing things. Henry Ford of the Ford motor industry in the USA, was one of these. He said that he had limited education but had vision and imagination to build an eight-cylinder engine cast in one block, something he was told couldn't be done. Engineers repeatedly said it was impossible, but after 18 months the engineers found a way to do it. How many of you now drive an eight-cylinder Ford vehicle? Henry Ford's vision and imagination demonstrates that if you can visualise and imagine it, you can do it. If you have a high score on this trait then do not be afraid to use it. BE PROUD OF YOUR BIG BUMPS on your head!

The "originality" trait (Fig B) is identified with the high mound in the middle of the forehead, under the hairline. People with this trait are also known as good original thinkers. They will have great ideas when no one else has thought of anything or are having trouble coming up with any ideas. The gift of intuition is the innate ability to know things instinctively without anyone even telling you. Women, particularly, have highly developed intuition. They will know when walking into a room who is with whom, who likes whom and who has fallen out with someone, even though they may say nothing. Looks, expression, the movement of the eyes and body language give away many secrets and women are usually very quick to pick up on it. It is good to exercise the gift of intuition and listen to it. Good intuition and originality are therefore go hand in hand.

To get your intuition working for you, ask yourself several questions and see how you feel about the answers. When confronted with a situation you're not too sure about or meeting an individual you don't really know, listen to your feelings. They will tell you all you need to know. Listen to how people talk, watch them closely. You might ask "if this were a garment, what would it feel like?'. You may also ask "if this was a piece of fruit, what would it taste like – sweet, bitter or tasteless?" By comparing situations to things we know, our senses quickly come into play and will give us the feeling about a situation.

The softer the area in the centre of the forehead where we find this trait, the more sensitive the person is in nature and temperament and usually more careful.

IMPATIENCE, PATIENCE, CONCENTRATION

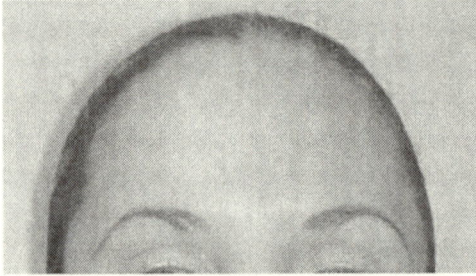

Fig A Impatience low concentration

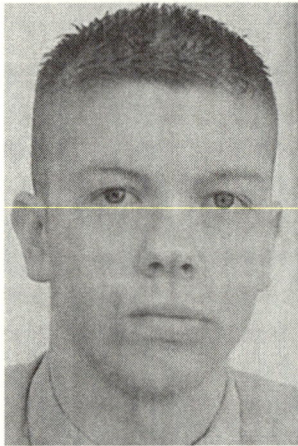

Fig B Patience and good concentration

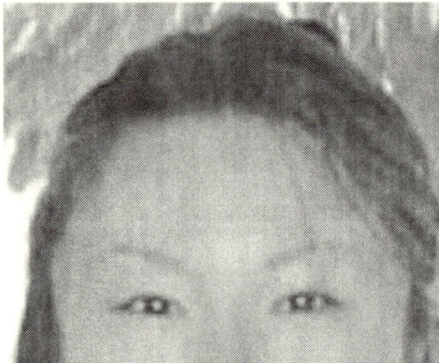

Fig C Conflicting traits
Very tolerant but extremely impatient!

The traits of impatience and patience are identified by the angle of the forehead. People with inward-sloping foreheads (Fig A) have a tendency to be very impatient. They will get agitated, waiting only a few moments as they want everything done yesterday. This can irritate you when you want to take your time, especially when they stand close behind you as if to hurry you along and you hear them tutting, sighing and muttering to themselves, "My God what's wrong with them". Everything to them should be done right now and as quickly as possible. They tend to welcome a break and look eagerly towards seeing the finish of a project. Yet they may be the complete opposite when they are doing things they want to take time with. They will often comment about others as being impatient yet don't see themselves as such. In fact, they will often try to convince you they are very patient! They have low concentration and tend to get sidetracked easily.

The opposite to this are those with horizontal and outward foreheads (front view as seen in Fig B) These people are very patient and have excellent concentration. People who have partners, or parents who have children with traits of high concentration should remember the thinking process of these individuals. They're like a large vehicle or Boeing 747 airliner that needs distance and time to stop. They have to gear down, so to speak. They can't just stop and walk away from a task. Knowing this, parents and partners should give a 10 to 15 minute warning to tell them that lunch is ready or whatever it is they want to get their attention.

Teachers as well as parents often chastise these children for disobedience and failing to come when called. It's, in fact, the individual who doesn't understand the trait for high concentration and how it affects people who possess this trait. They need time to gear down and pace themselves ready for the next procedure. Impatient people can drop everything there and then and change or stop what they are doing with ease, but getting them to concentrate on a job for any length of time can be a problem. The way to overcome this is by assigning a task, making it interesting or having frequent breaks. They tend to start back on the task with refreshed zeal.

In Oriental races, we often find a conflicting trait combination of impatience and high tolerance (Fig C).
Very wide-set eyes = **extremely tolerant**
Inward sloping forehead = **very impatient**

This conflicting trait is best described as follows. If this person had the same food every mealtime, three times a day for a month she would willingly accept it, and would never complain, as she is very tolerant. But if she had to wait more than a minute for it she would become very frustrated and agitated and start to complain. This is known as "impatience in the moment". This trait is seen in many Oriental races. If your partner has this trait, you can often do the same things over and over again and they will never complain. But don't be late or you're in big trouble!

Impatient people are great for hosting meetings as they get things over quickly. They work quickly and want to complete the job. If there is a deadline, they'll make sure they hit it. Patient people are good in positions such as teachers and doctors who have to deal with others and make them feel at ease.

PEOPLE, INFORMATION AND THINGS

Fig A

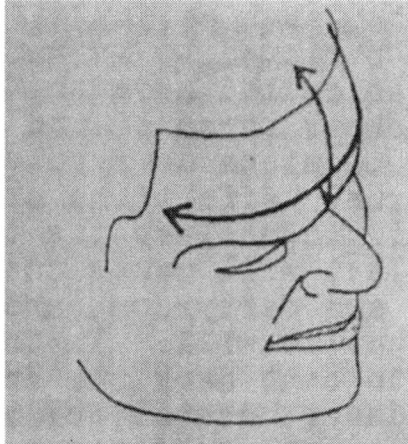

Fig B
People and things

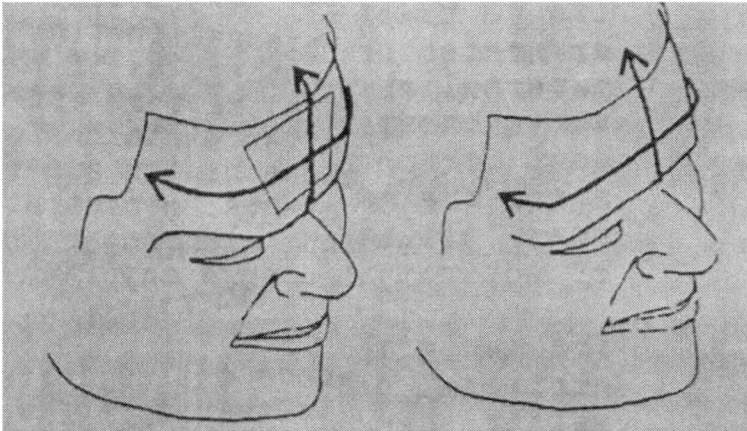

Fig C
Information

Fig D
Things rather than people

The forehead indicates what we are more interested in.

Fig A shows the gift to remember information, also illustrated in Fig C. It's obvious to see as it appears as if they have a flat spot or area. They love information and like to hold information about projects and data. They make good doctors, lawyers and are good in any profession that requires holding detailed information. The more vertical (side profile view) the forehead is, the greater the ability to hold information and have good recall.

A vertical indentation (Fig B) in forehead between the eyebrows. shows the person likes specific things and prefers working on specific projects rather than working with people. He will be happy to work on his own and get engrossed in the project. Another interesting thing to note here is that when you see sharp vertical lines going up the forehead ABOVE the eyebrows, then these people like to do everything by the book. If you see the lines start to go off at a 45% angle, for example, these are people who outwardly go by the book but will look for every opportunity to bend the rules, depending on the angle of the line.

Fig D illustrates that people with this type of forehead – wide and what we call a "construction" type head – would rather be working on a project or thing and not alongside others. They will work well with others but want to get on with their own project and will get totally engrossed in it. When assigning jobs to individuals, it's good to look at the forehead. Fig B is better able to work with people in businesses involving people and services.

Fig C are those who are found in medical professions, research, accounts and law and such like, where a good head for information is required.

Fig D are drawn to engineering, mechanics, construction and building careers. A good rule to remember is that round heads are for those better working with people, square heads are for those who work better on things and projects.

An easy way to remember how to identify what a person is interested in is this rule of thumb:

Round forehead:
Loves working with people.
Any customer services type jobs.

Round forehead with a vertical indent:
Loves working with people and on a specific task or project.
Likes working in a team on a project.

Round forehead with flat spot in middle:
Loves people and information.
Likes working with people such as librarian, teaching, medical.

Round forehead with flat spot and vertical indent:
Loves working with people and projects as well as information.
Example, scientific team on specific projects or engineering.

Flat forehead with indent:
Loves information and things, rather than working with people.
Mechanics, construction, on specific projects or fields.

Flat forehead:
Loves working on projects and things, rather than with people.
Anything that they can do on their own – farming, driving, fishing, forestry etc.

INTELLECT

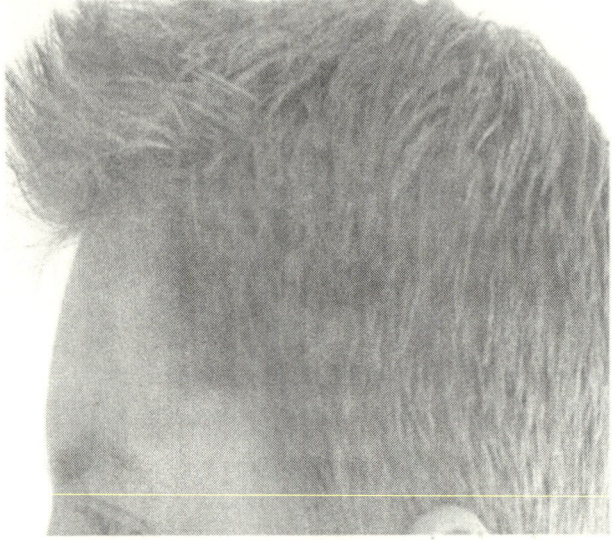

Fig A
High intellect

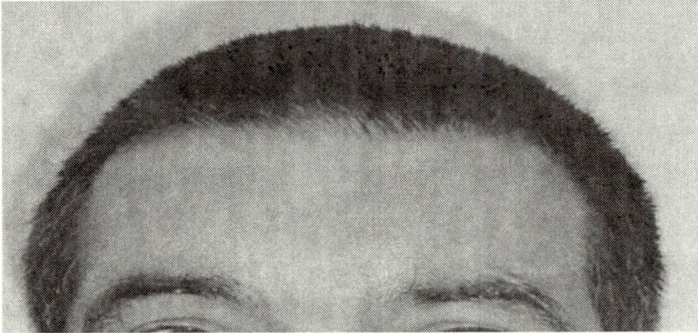

Fig B
Low intellect

HIGH INTELLECT

Intellect is measured by the height of the forehead. THIS HAS NOTHING TO DO WITH INTELLIGENCE, it is simply the matter of being able to determine QUALITY OF INFORMATION REQUIRED TO STIMULATE THE BRAIN."

A high forehead is an indication of high intellect (Fig A). People with this tend to be what we might call abstract thinkers. They prefer intellectual subjects to stimulate the brain and get irritated with trivial or small talk. They can tend to isolate themselves. Children who have a high intellect will often be loners and draw away from associating from other children, feeling they have nothing in common with them. Parents with children of high intellect should cultivate this ability by giving them good books and projects to do and things that stimulate the mind whilst also encouraging them to mix with others. If they do not have this mental stimulation they can grow up to be very mentally frustrated. This is often a reason why some turn delinquent and get into trouble for no apparent reason, much to the surprise of the parents. It has been found that many young offenders are, in fact, very bright and have some excellent gifts in their traits, but these were never cultivated by parents. This left the child mentally frustrated and agitated.

One young female offender had some amazing gifts for problem-solving, high intellect, originality and imagination, yet the court barred her from entering a city centre for three years due to repeated offences. If those who were supposed to be taking care of her, such as the social services, had been aware of this, she may not have got into the situation in the first place and could have been directed into a meaningful, well-paid career and later become credit to the community.

LOW INTELLECT

Shorter fore-headed people are inclined to have a low intellect (as seen in Fig B). These people prefer general information and small talk and may feel uncomfortable with more intellectual conversation. They don't see a need for it. They are not interested, for example, in science and mathematics, UFOs and deep subjects that can be heavy going and require research and study. They will talk about such subjects but with just a passing interest and then move on to other things. Trivial and everyday mundane things tend to be the big highlights in their life, often referred to as a "soap opera" mentality.

Couples with conflicting levels of intellect, as well as interests, will find they will be like two goats or rams butting each other every time they have a conversation or socialise. They will both want to talk about completely different subjects and choose a completely different circle of friends, each other's choice irritating the other.

The consideration of the trait "intellect" is a serious matter when one is considering making a commitment to a long-term relationship or marriage, as many a couple has found out, after they signed the marriage certificate. Failure to consider this can result in each person going his own way, seeking compatible associates and, in some cases, resulting in an affair because they feel they have nothing in common with their partner. All the pain and hurt that is reaped from such situations could have been avoided if they had been given this information before they made a commitment.

METHODICAL, DETAILED CONCERN, EXACTNESS

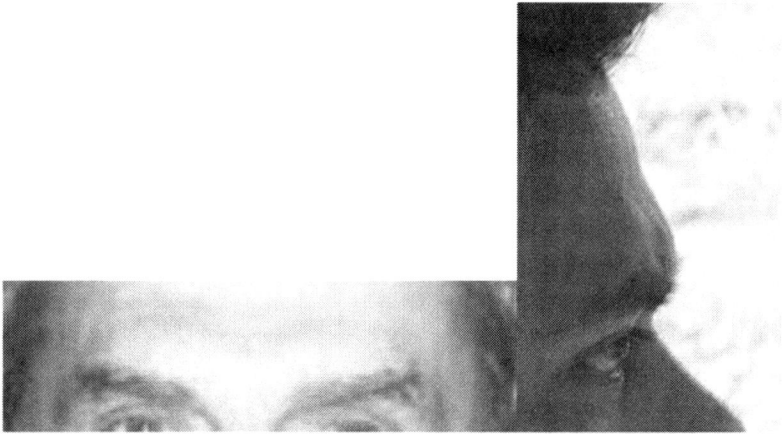

Fig A   Fig B
Methodical - A mound across the brow. Front and side views

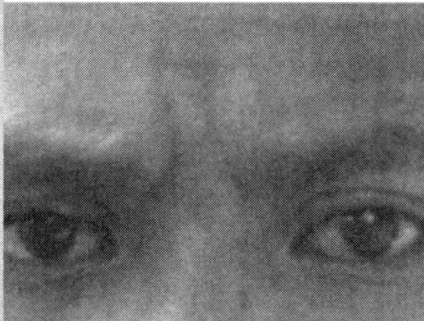

Fig C   Fig D

A horizontal, prominent ridge above the eyebrows (Fig A, B and C) shows that the person is methodical, is a person of habit who does things by routine and is predictable. An example of this trait can be seen in military personal who tend to have the same agenda each day. They have a place for everything, neatness and order are a strict must for them and they get agitated and upset if it is not so. These people like to hold to a strict routine and have a set way to do everything. Everything is carried out in a formal step-by-step manner and they will tend to develop a habitual approach to all things. They are people who like to follow procedure and go by the book. Others may not be so formal but still develop the trait due to the brain going through the same strict routine day-after-day. Under control it's a great trait, but one must remember that the home should be a home, not a parade ground for strict military precision which will exasperate and demoralise family members if they are expected to live as if it were.

Mounds over the inner eyebrows (Fig D) are known as "Detail concern or Exactness", found in people who have a habitual obsession with detail and getting things right. Vertical lines in the forehead by the inner eyebrow are caused by concentration and found in individuals who spend a lot of time concentrating on projects that require precise and accurate focus. From dentists and surgeons, to engineers and draftsman, you will see the manifestation of this trait showing that the person needs to habitually focus on detail, with high concentration.

IDEALISTIC AND RESOLUTE

Fig A
Idealistic

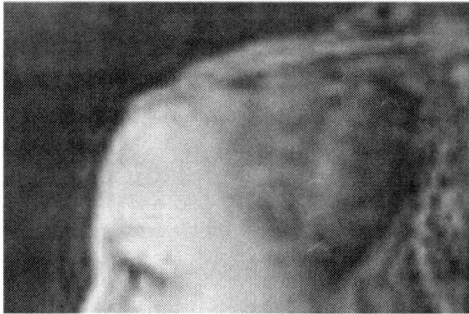

Fig B
Resolute

IDEALISM

When a person has a head where the middle is higher than the fore-head and also the back of the head they are completely idealistic as shown in Fig A. In other words, instead of the slope of the head running from the back of the head downwards to the front, or the slope of the head going from the fore-head downwards toward the back, the head appears to meet in the middle, sloping evenly in both directions.

Such people are dreamers, living in a fantasy world, are unrealistic in approaching real-life situations, dream about everything and usually do very little, as most of the time they are planning, dreaming or fanaticising about how things should be or as they would like to see it. This is a rare sight to see and few people have this trait but when you see it, the head shape just looks a little odd. If the trait is out of control, they come across as the nicest people you would ever like to meet, but getting them to think soundly and logically can be a real challenge. They can sometimes make you feel as if all the lights are on, but nobody is home! Or the engine's running but no one's behind the wheel. This trait is one that, when used with a balanced view, can be a great advantage as these people have an idea and will go to great lengths to get others to follow and make the dream into a reality. Such men as Lincoln, Washington and Franklyn were men of great idealism.

On the other hand, other men have become unbalanced and behaved like bullying tyrants who seek to use force to get others to submit to their ideals and whims. Some exert racialism and other ideologies and then try to force this onto everyone they come in contact with. When all's said and done, we should be open to any idea and suggestion, as long as it doesn't encroach upon the rights of others or brings others' lives into a path of suffering, when the ideal should be to create a better quality of life for all. Ambition as a trait is basically selfish in that it only seeks the personal ideals and goals of the individual. The spirit of aspiration, on the other hand, involves working for greater things and for greater benefit of the many, not just for self. In this regard, many men with great idealism and opportunity, who have become leaders, have completely and miserably failed. They have not kept this trait in line with sound logic, reasonableness and compassionate thinking toward others which has resulted in much grief to mankind.

RESOLUTE

This trait is identified by the sharp right-angle of forehead (side view Fig B). The fore-head looks a bit like a square brick. This trait is called "resolute", meaning the person is not open to new ideas, does not like to change his viewpoint, is set in his ways and will not accept alternate views on things. Even when shown improved data, evidence, proof and all the facts, he will still hold onto old, out-of-date ideas and his old rigid opinion. He can come across as totally unreasonable when changes are required to move forward, and he is unwilling to budge an inch or move even on minor issues or things.

They are often referred to as people who are "set in their ways" or as a "stick in the mud". Persons who have this trait must remember that to progress and move forward, they have to change thinking and views from time to time. This in no way means that they have to compromise on values or principles. It simply means that they have to keep up with new knowledge and research and be open to new suggestions. Persons who have a high score in "resolute" are by nature more stable in their outlook as they hold on to sets of principles and a standard from which they will not budge.

Having said this, we have to know where to set the boundaries and guidelines, as it can also result in pointless stubbornness, in which little progress can be made in dealing with issues. Being balanced and having reasonableness in all things should be a guiding factor if you're prone to be resolute. Again, the positive side is that persons who have good morals and principles are not easily influenced by others and will stick to their principles no matter what – something which is greatly lacking in this liberated age of today.

PERSONAL NOTES

PERSONAL NOTES

PERSONAL NOTES

PERSONAL NOTES

THE FACE

ASYMMETRY OF THE FACE

When asymmetry occurs in any trait, there will be a mood swing in that area. The more asymmetry seen in the face, the more complex the person can be. The more mood swings a person has can result in the individual being vulnerable to becoming unstable and also unpredictable. A high percentage of criminals have extreme asymmetry in the face.

A close examination of police and prison mug-shots will confirm this. Judge Jones believed that every crime was associated with asymmetry, due to the unstable and unpredictable behaviour resulting from such mood swings. As they say it's not a matter of "do you love the person?" but more "can you live with the mood swings" of the person, because both men and woman who have extreme asymmetry can also be extremely difficult to live with.

What Judge Jones also discovered was that the dominant traits in any of the trait areas of the face, if they are out of control, will be a positive factor in why people are drawn or feel a tendency to go in a certain direction toward a negative and destructive course if not corrected. In other words, a person with a trait of high risk-taking, if not given the correct direction into sports or creative adventure such a motor racing, climbing, sky-diving, bungee jumping or whatever, will seek the same thrill and adrenalin rush from doing other things to create the feelings, be it criminal or otherwise. It's for this reason that so many offenders do have some amazing gifts and good traits. We say that bad as the problem is, it is only good traits that have gone out of control. By knowing the dominant traits of our own face and our children's – both the positive and negative sides – we can foresee the possible problems before they come to the surface and can take action to redirect the course for positive good, rather than reap the sad results from poor self-discipline. When we have serious mood swings, we can also understand why we may suddenly feel the need to go on a certain course, in some cases an extreme from what we would call conventional behaviour and which would not be acceptable. This would then be unconventional behaviour. Judge Jones would use the principle of elimination. Who would be the most likely person to commit a particular crime if his traits were out of control? As he studied the faces of offenders standing before him in a court, he began to see how this knowledge was able to allow him predict the crime the offender had committed, before they'd even opened their mouths.

Because the tendency is for traits to automatically go on a negative or destructive path if left without direction, this is why close supervision and discipline of children is so very important if you want them to grow up model citizens with sound minds. Lack of discipline or guidance would be like a large sailing ship left with no one standing at the helm to steer it. It's of interest to note that such positive directions was written down long ago by ancient wise King Solomon, Jesus Christ and even Buddha –

"Train up a boy according to the way for him, even when he grows old he will not turn aside from it"
Proverbs chapter 22 verse 6.

"Because sentence against a bad worker has not been executed speedily, that is why the heart of the sons of men has become fully set in them to do bad"
King Solomon's words at Ecclesiastes chapter 8 verse 11.

"Whatever a man sows, this he will also reap"
Jesus Christ

"All are the result of what we have thought""
Buddha (563 BCE – 483 BDC)

Feeding the mind with wholesome thoughts is like the correct fertilizer for what you want to grow so that it becomes a part of you, your very make up and personality. If you feed your mind on gratuitous violence, sex perversion, hatred, racialism, greed, selfish ambition, coveting, anger, jealousy and malice, you will create another person just like many we see today who ruin peaceful everyday life.

Carpenters use razor-sharp tools, from chisels to saws, yet they don't go about cutting the limbs of others. Chefs also use knives and cleavers everyday but neither do have the desire to attack others and dismember them. So knives do not kill people, it is people who kill people. And no matter what traits an individual may have, a gifted man can kill if his traits are out of control, whereas a man not so gifted will still make for himself a good, peaceful life, because he feeds his mind healthily thoughts and sets his heart to do so.

Recognizing our own personal traits and what will bring out the best in us, is the first step; second is feeding the mind with constructive, wholesome, thinking subject material that will cultivate these traits so that we become unique and we are able to contribute what we have. Yes, to give each of us the very best of character development to the enjoyment of both ourselves and others.

If asymmetry is a problem then the safest route is always the calm one: to keep stress to a minimum so as not to trigger off extreme reactions and behaviour. Take a path that always keeps you relaxed and in a calm disposition. The following page shows examples of couples to illustrate those with non-matching traits who will have children suffering mood swings – some with possibly serious mood swings. To see if you are compatible, you can get photos, looking face on to the camera, as seen by our examples, and cut them in half and try to match up both of your faces. This will give you a very good idea if your traits are similar or conflicting.

151

EXAMPLES OF GENETIC MATCHES AND HOW THEY CAN AFFECT COMPATIBILITY AND CHILDREN

Bad match   Bad match   Good match

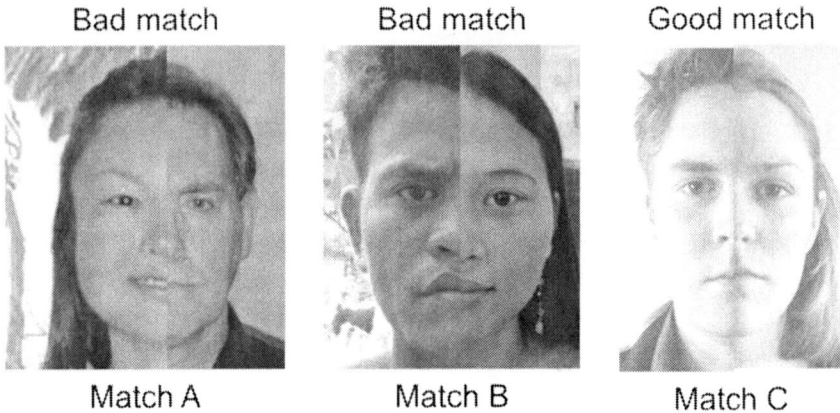

Match A   Match B   Match C

Simply cut your photo in half and place it alongside your partner's. If you appear like A or B, you are more likely to have many conflicts in your relationship and have children with possibly serious mood swings leading to potential problems. If you are already married, or in a relationship, you will now understand how to handle these traits thus avoiding many conflicts.

If you resemble match C, you have very good prospects of being happy for many years and have children with low mood swings.

The examples shown here illustrate how traits can affect asymmetry with the width of the face and forehead and it is interesting to note that the authentic couple on the right "C" said they never argue and agreed on almost everything as their traits were so well-matched. The closer the genetic traits match, the greater the prospect of a happy relationship and long-term partnership which will easily blend together.

Matches A and B are used as an example only is to illustrate the point. If they were real couples they would face many challenges if they had a relationship. If they had children, they would have serious mood swings. Match C has good matching traits and is compatible in most areas. If they have children they will have far fewer or low mood swings.

The majority of couples have no idea and can't foresee the potential challenges of entering a relationship and wanting to have children. It's too late once children arrive. Parents may not understand why the school authorities may from time to time call them in for a chat about the conduct of their child and his or her unpredictable, unconventional behaviour, which makes them disruptive in class and very difficult to handle. Parents need to be kind yet firm with discipline so the child grows to know what is automatically right for him to do. If they have this direction from early age, they will do the right thing by second nature. This is what King Solomon was referring to in the previous quote. The traits and gifts children have should be gently directed to build a wonderful, stable, positive personality that others will truly admire and love.

If children have mood swings, they will take this with them into adulthood and if they are serious or extreme, they will grow up to be very complex individuals. Unless they seek some help or understand the cause of such mixed feelings, emotions and temperaments, they will suffer agitation, frustration and even aggression which they may take out on others due to the stress and inward turmoil.

One such man, who suffered from extreme asymmetry in the face, said that he would be in prison by now if it were not for counselling and meditation to keep himself calm and learn how to cope with his temperament and mood swings. Again, if there is a mood swing in any trait area, the safest way is to take the calm route, not letting yourself get into a situation that is going to cause you undue discomfort and stress. This may be intolerance, impatience, restlessness and criticalness, for example. It's a fact that we all have mood swings, but keeping them under control is what is important so they don't take over our lives and ruin our peace and peace of those around us.

The following pages illustrate Judge Jones's research that found serious asymmetry in traits resulted in complex, unstable characters who had a tendency to commit crimes. In nearly all cases extreme asymmetry can be seen in the faces of the offenders. There are thousands of mug-shots such as these examples that were sent to me by Dr Paul B Elsner.

Unconventional behaviour is high on the trait list with offenders. Nearly all the mug-shots shown here indicate a high score for being unconventional, meaning that those pictured will find it difficult to conform and will take a different path from the norm. Fitting into society would be a challenge, since they would automatically do the opposite of what was expected in rational thought.

It certainly makes one think that, if all these offenders were given the help they really needed at an early age, would they have found themselves standing before a judge listening to their sentence being handed out? Likewise today, the computer games industry is fuelling the minds of so many of today's youth, and even the very young, with violence, killing and fighting games, that they are totally unaware their minds have become desensitised. Is it any wonder why they react and do the things they do? When the film industry, TV and the press swamp us with sex, killing and hardcore scenes of brutality is it any wonder that we live in a society that turns to violence and stabbings when confronted with situations where an individual's traits should automatically stand by good, wholesome principles? Instead they automatically go into a negative mood and take to the path that will lead to more heartache and trouble.

As mentioned, a child playing an instrument doesn't play bad notes, he or she just plays notes that are sometimes in the wrong place. Remember, whatever your traits are, **STUDY THEM WELL** so that you know why you may feel like taking a certain path or want to do a particular thing. Secondly, cultivate good thinking habits about wholesome, positive, healthy things. If you do this, then you improve your world and the world around you. Further, if you do this, you will never find yourself in a regrettable position of being asked by a judge, "How do you plead, guilty or not guilty". Or hearing the words echoed in your head for many years "You have been sentenced to serve…".

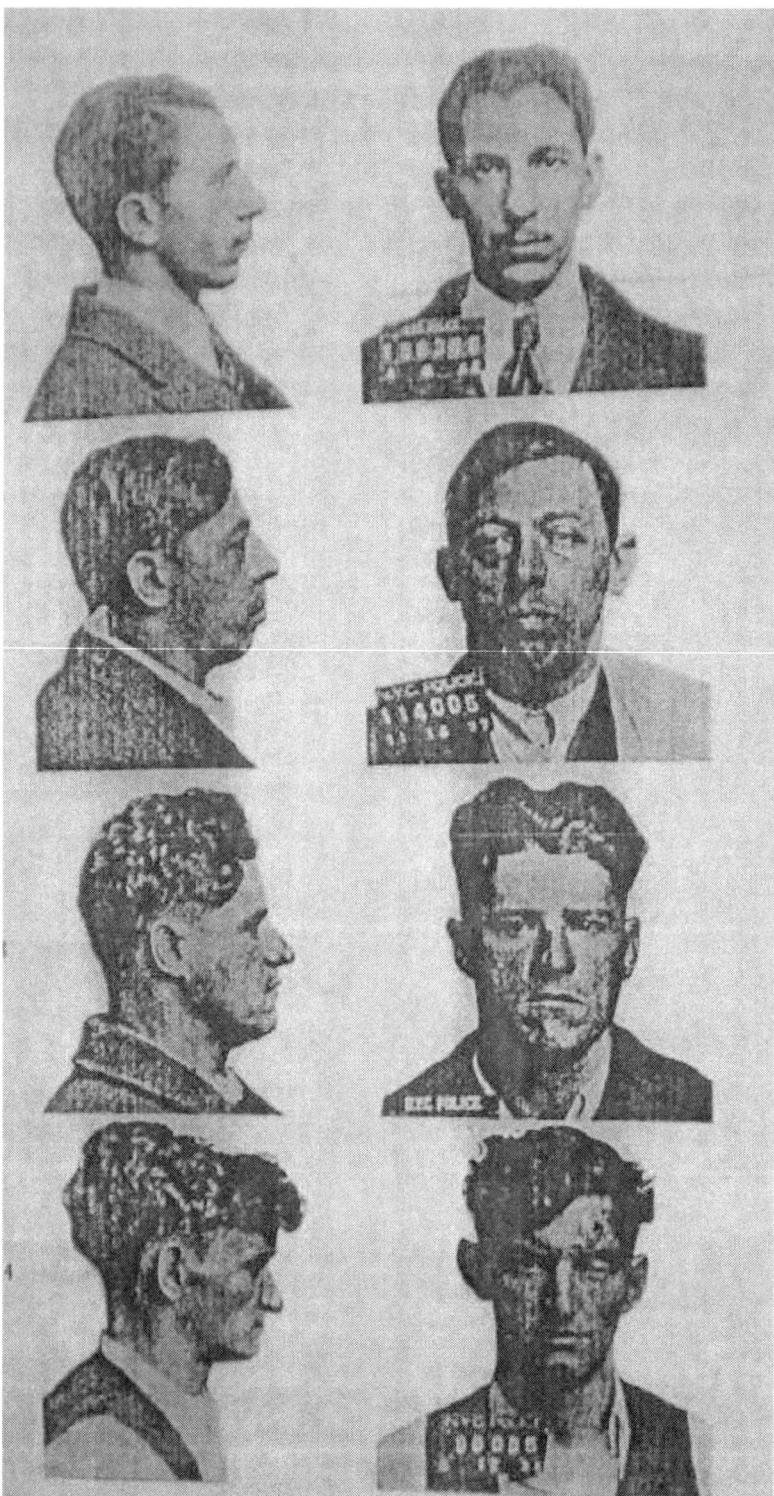

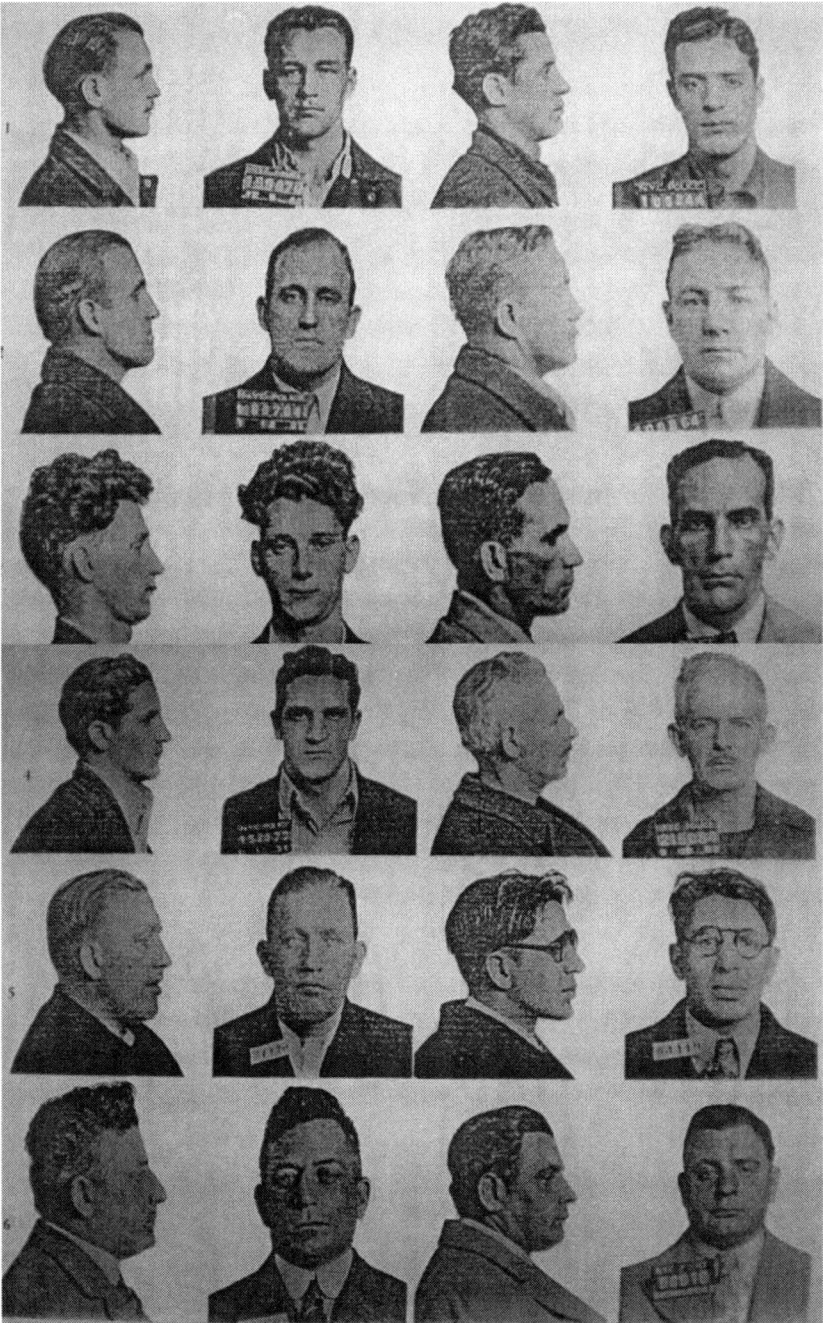

Can you spot the trait — unconventional eyes out of line

ENVIRONMENTAL, AND OTHER TRAITS

Some traits are not inherited but caused by a person's own thinking, living style and their environment.

An example of an environmental trait is the permanent frown, probably from taking things too seriously. It makes people look as if they are agitated or angry when they may not be. A squint in the eyes is a sign of those who are shifty in nature and somewhat distrusting.

Lines in the forehead reveal our thinking pattern and a give away what is going on in our heads before we open our mouths. Lines running from nostrils to the side of mouth are described as oral lines. The deeper the lines, the more effect there is on an expression or the deeper the individual's thoughts behind their words. These people speak as if every word counts. Other traits relating to the mouth have also been observed, such as those who have teeth that appear to turn inward. Those with this trait will tend to hold feelings in and are good at holding secrets and keeping confidentiality, whereas those with protruding teeth will tell everyone your secrets and find difficulty in keeping confidentiality.

As more and more studies are undertaken in human nature, the more we can understand who we are. The more knowledge we have the greater the success of keeping peace between one another but…. ***only if we apply what we learn!***

Some other traits of interest are the lines of the face…

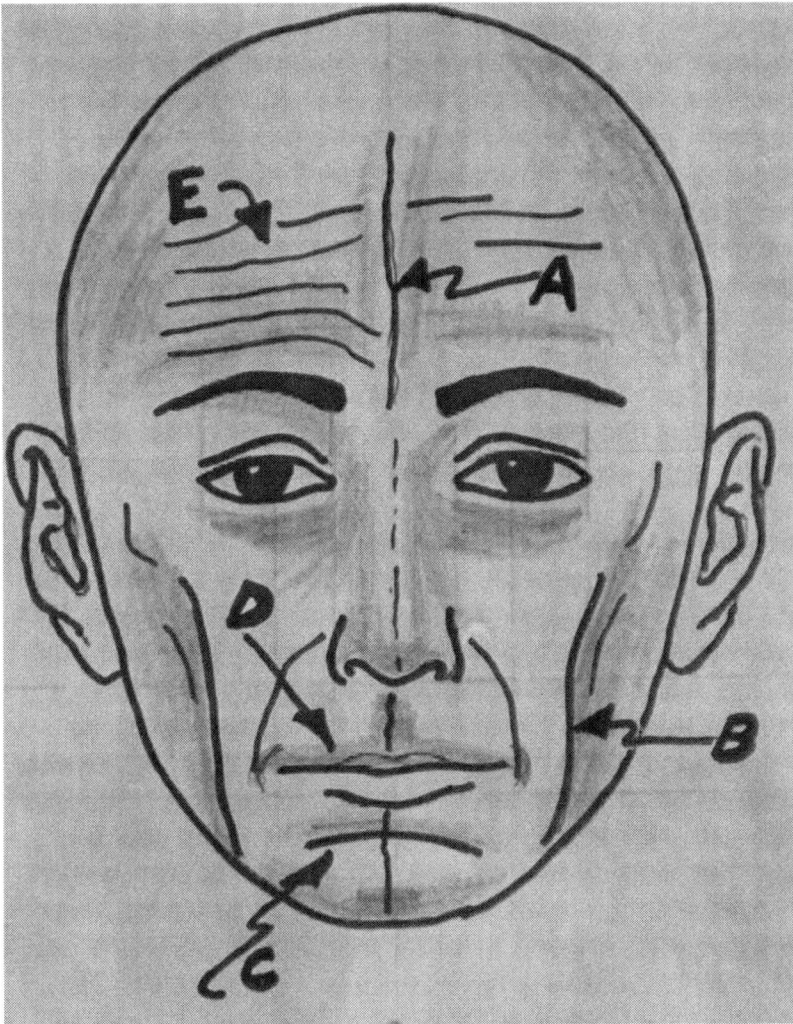

Environmental lines of the face are caused by several things – happiness, stress or our thinking and attitude. Laughter-lines around the eyes are common when people smile and laugh a lot. As already mentioned they are called "crows'-feet". But when we look closely, we can sometimes see the signs of severe grief, pain or suffering. In the face drawn here we have marked a few of these. A is where there appears as if there is a line like a tear down the middle of the face. Sometimes it's sharp and other times a little jagged. This is where the face looks as if the skin has been torn in two. What causes this?

159

We explain this as a sign that the brain is torn in two, going in completely different directions and with strong mixed feelings and emotions. All the muscles are continually tugging to and fro. For example, a woman may desire a beautiful home, husband and a family. After she is given this she becomes pregnant, has a family and lacks nothing. But she's married to a man she just does not love, as it was a marriage pre-arranged by the parents. No matter what she does, she feels her heart torn apart, living in a marriage she really wanted with children she so much desired, a home she wants to enjoy, but with the wrong man. She wanted to marry the man of her dreams but due to pressure from the family, religious culture and so on, she was forced to accept a pre-arranged marriage.

A man might for example find his perfect job and after years of training and waiting, gets his big break. He gets a great career and can be very successful and has everything he needs, with good pay and benefits. But he's working in a city he really loathes. He hates the travelling each day and works with people he doesn't like. On one hand he has everything he wants to support his family, on the other hand he totally hates the situation, location and environment and but can't get out of it. He also knows he will have to stay put for years due to a contract. The inner turmoil he may suffer can eventually show itself in the face as a tear line. This trait has often been seen in people who have suffered financial turmoil in business. If you see this trait, for whatever reason, it's an indication that the person has undergone great internal, mental and emotional turmoil where the mind has been pulled in two very different directions at the same time.

Line B is another trait caused by severe stress and emotional grief. It is where the cheeks look as if they have been pulled in and a tear line often appears down the face. When looking at faces of people who were born during the war periods, the men appeared to be very hard and children born from these fathers would suffer severe discipline with little love or affection. It's as if they were bullied, beaten or slapped and then told: "don't you dare cry or you'll get another slap". The child holds in the emotions, pulling in the cheek muscles. Over years this develops into a line or crease. People having this trait give an indication that they have had a very hard or difficult childhood, with little or no affection.

Area C also indicates that the person holds in grief and doesn't allow himself to cry or express emotions. This can develop or cause a tear line in the chin right on the top of the ball of the chin under the bottom lip. It can also look like a scar or as if they have had a cut at one time.

D is another tell-tale sign of an individual who has suffered great emotional stress in childhood. The lips by birth are sharp and the edge of the top lip is sharply defined and can be almost like a corner. The more stress put on a person, especially when they are a child, will pull the lips round and the muscles will cause the lips to lose this sharp edge and it appears as if there's no edge at all and the lips look undefined. The turmoil of holding in tears and the fear of letting go or expressing their emotions, from fear of further ill-treatment is the cause of this trait. Many victims of abuse will often show this trait, in some cases in quite an extreme way, as if there is no top lip definition at all. A sharp top lip definition is usually a good sign of a happier childhood.

When meeting people who have these traits, it's good to remember that, although they may appear sometimes to be harder in nature, underneath they may in fact be very sensitive. It is simply that they were never allowed to express their feelings and emotions and can come across in later life as somewhat cold, insensitive or hard in temperament. The opposite is often true. They are, in fact, very warm people, they just have trouble expressing their feelings, due to being oppressed for so many years or because they have suffered a very hard life emotionally.

E shows the common lines we often see in individual's foreheads. What do they tell us? As we think, we use muscles that are constantly moving in various directions. As time goes by we start to develop thought pattern lines. This in itself is a big subject, but to explain briefly, if you see the lines level (or horizontal) going right across the forehead it's an indication of the thought pattern being balance with little variation in thinking. As we get older, the lines will tend to alter or break. If, for example, a person becomes more philosophical, and what might be termed spiritual thinking or higher thinking, the lines will start to go upwards in a slant toward the middle. If a person who is earthly in thinking, for example, he likes to think of indulging himself in animalistic pursuits, sex, gluttonous living, drink, or is crude, vulgar and obscene, you will see these line go downward when going across to the middle. The same is true when one is totally physical and dogmatic. Everything is "bang, bang, bang; this is that, this is this", what might be called mentally fist thumping on the table. It can often be seen as several big "V" lines between the eyes.

Again, when one has followed a thought pattern for some time and then becomes aware of a change of thought the lines will show breaks, as if going in a completely different direction. When you see these breaks, you know that something has happened to cause the individual to completely change their thinking. People who have been brought up, for example, in religious cults with extremes of religious, controlled thinking and then find they have been deceived or mislead, will change their entire thinking process. Their new way of thinking will start new lines, making those on the forehead look as if they have been broken and new ones will start a few millimetres above or below them. If the forehead has a mass of broken lines, then the person may have rather an unstable mentality, with his line of thought constantly changing from one thing to another and never settled in any specific way of thinking. As the subject of lines in the forehead is another deep study, we'll just mention a few basic things to help understand a little more about them. If you see any of the lines discussed here, it's good to be discreet when talking to an individual and asking about them. By letting the individual tell you a little about their life and changes of direction, you will soon understand what has caused these lines to appear in their face. A simple question might be: "Do you find that over the years you have changed your views and thinking pattern on…?" If they say "yes", you might then ask: "what made you change your views on…?". You will soon see the lines begin to make sense.

When reading a face for someone you need to take into account when dealing with others such things as botox and other cosmetic treatments. It's a good idea to ask any individual who wants you to read their traits if they have had any cosmetic treatment, as this can affect the accuracy of your reading. A person with a large hooked nose, who has had surgery, could now appear with a ski jump nose, or a person with a receding chin may appear to be very tenacious with his new protruding chin. Yet the traits do not change if one has cosmetic surgery. In such cases, an original photo of the individual must be consulted and viewed. When reading other people's faces, just remember to be discreet as they may want any surgery held in strict confidence in front of others. A professionally trained personologist will take all these things into consideration.

LOOKING FOR YOUR IDEAL PARTNER

Do you know what to look for in your ideal partner, who will suit you and what are the six basic traits you should consider? EVERYONE ENTERING A RELATIONSHIP SHOULD READ THIS INFORMATION.

The following information explains why these six traits are so important in long-term relationships and the potential problems which may occur if we ignore them. We trust that by reading the basic information in this book, you will have a better idea of who you are and what to look for in a partner. You will soon learn what these traits mean. You will soon become a good communicator and understanding listener and your relationships will greatly improve. As regards finding an ideal partner you will know exactly what to look for. You will know almost immediately you meet someone if they will be a suitable partner or not. This will save you much frustration, repeated disappointment and will avoid time-wasting. If you are already in a relationship, this information will also help you understand who you and your partner really are.

What will you look for?
Handsome, beautiful, a nice figure, great body, wealthy, has money, is popular, has good job?

WRONG! These things may be of some importance but they don't take into consideration the basic building blocks of a relationship that will last.

Consider this too. Why do people with good jobs and careers; professional people with good education and wealth, still finish up in a divorce court? Why is the divorce rate the same if not more in a wealthy, successful society? Why is it that people who may be poor or have little education, still find happiness and build a life with a partner that lasts for many years? Simply because even though educated, most people still lack the basic understanding of who they are and what is needed for a good match when choosing a partner.

There are six basic things needed for compatibility for a happy relationship to work reasonably smoothly and most people do not know what these are, let alone think about them. By choosing a partner similar to ourselves, although it may appear that opposites attract, at the end of the day the longer-lasting relationships are those that have matching traits, NOT opposite ones. Strange as this may seem, it's absolutely true. These traits can be easily handled when we understand how. The first thing we really need to understand is the basic building blocks needed for a successful relationship.

Here are six basic traits you must consider and which are all explained in this book

1. <u>Physical Insulation or Temperament</u>. A person's sensitivity is assessed by measuring an individual's hair thickness, NOT if it's light or dark, but more importantly whether it is very fine or thick. Read the section under **"Hair"** to understand how hair thickness affects people's sensitivity and compatibility with each other.

2. <u>Tolerance</u>. This is affected by the width between the eyes – narrow or wide. What is the depth of eyes? Are they overly serious or too flippant? Read the section under eyes to see how conflicting **"Tolerance"** can result in serious conflict in relationships.

3. <u>Intellect. Basic education and background</u>. Frustration and poor communication can result if this aspect is ignored. Men tend to overlook this matter and women will suffer feelings of loneliness and isolation if they can't talk and communicate with a partner who has poor education, or has little interest in intellectual things. The reverse also applies. Read the section on **"Intellect"** to understand why you should consider this trait before making a commitment in a relationship.

4. <u>Leg length</u>. Short legs are more active while longer legs more inclined to sit at a desk job. Even if interested in sport, individuals will vary in what they will be active in. Read section on **"Legs"** to see how different leg length can cause conflict in relationships.

5. <u>Width of the face, head shape and thinking process.</u> Wide will tend to be confident; more narrow will tend to gain confidence with knowledge although not naturally confident. The thinking process can cause huge problems if couples don't match. Read the whole sections on the **"Face"** and **"Forehead"**

6. <u>Similar interest</u>. This will depend on shape of head, interest in people, information or in things and projects. If there is any conflict here, then the relationship will definitely suffer as one will feel isolated while the other is enjoying what they want to do. Again, read the information on **"Head"** shape so as to understand why conflicts can arise if there is not compatible.

Although these may appear to be insignificant factors in a relationship, they are in fact very important. Disagreements, even heated arguments and fights, can erupt if one has a partner with conflicting traits.

Love is blind, as they say, and few people realise the potential problems of having interests that are not only different but very conflicting with their partner's. A people friendly person who loves to have friends and entertain, chatting and socializing, will find it hard sharing time with a partner who is only interested in things and projects and likes to potter about on his own and doesn't like company.

Although each individual has the right to his own space and should respect another's choice (because we all need time to ourselves), over time this may become a reason for drifting apart if they cannot agree to do some things together. Spending time together early in the relationship will feel comfortable, but as time goes by and a couple get to know each other, they may find they will argue where to spend time and who with. If they can't agree, it's inevitable they will drift apart and one partner may in time seek out company from someone else, which may result in an affair and break-up of the relationship, bringing unpleasantness to all involved. The whole situation could have been avoided if they had sat down and calculated the potential problems before making the commitment.

Other things to be considered are background and culture if a partner is not of the same race. Religion, common values, personal habits, hygiene, as well as social habits and lifestyle, such as drinking, smoking, gambling and entertainment, also need to be considered as well as how they handle finances, or take responsibility. All these are factors that can seriously affect a relationship if not taken into consideration before making a commitment. When one marries a partner one not only marries the person *but also marries into the family or into a culture.*

One of the big problems today is, that with a liberated society, people are very quick to get involved in a sexual relationship. Once this occurs, people tend not to talk as they become so preoccupied with the physical relationship as well as pressure from a partner who may use emotional blackmail, if you are not engaging in sex – "You Don't Love Me"…or "You must have someone else". With all this going on, talking things through in many cases is brushed aside or even forgotten. Men are the worst offenders as they want the pleasure before ever counting the cost! The thing to remember is that everything in life has a price tag. We can get a great deal or reap a whole lot of trouble. Sitting down and talking could have avoided such trauma and deep regret.

DR PAUL B ELSNER –
his work and personology for schools

Dr Paul B Elsner knew Judge Jones personally and was involved with personology for around 60 years, His work was aimed at the school and education system where time and time again he found the same problems resulting from pupils using the wrong hand. For example, if they were born left-handed, parents would try to force them to use the right hand, thinking this was the right thing to do.

The findings on this were quite amazing and almost all the children, who were suffering what he called "Mixed Brain Dominance", had experienced the same difficulties. The result was that children were not able to do joined-up writing, were only able to print letters and also had great difficulty with mathematics, becoming confused and not grasping information, appearing to have mental blocks over simple things and dyslexia.

If Dr Elsner found the child appeared to be using the wrong hand, on consulting with many parents he advised them to change the handedness of the child, and encouraged them to use their birth dominant hand, and the problems began to rectify themselves. Although many in the education system – psychologists and the like – tried to dispute his findings, nevertheless the results he had were impressive and very successful. Before they could even open their mouths, Dr Elsner would look at the head shape of a child and by watching the child using their hand would immediately tell parents "Your child has trouble with writing, mathematics and possible dyslexia…am I right?" In nearly all cases the parent would agree. We mention this information because if your child is suffering from any of these learning difficulties, you may find the answer very simple – change the handedness from right to left or left to right. Try it! A battery inserted the wrong way round fails: simple! It was a massive problem with a very simple answer.

On the point of negative thinking, Judge Edward V Jones said that he was often hampered by the lack of support from many claiming to be so-called experts in their field, yet who failed to recognize some of his basic findings and the overwhelming evidence he discovered in his 20 years serving as a judge. Present-day personology has been validated by the scientific work of Judge Jones and Robert Whiteside.

With regard to using the wrong hand and what our birth handedness should be, one way to spot this was, according to Dr Elsner, by looking at the head and tilting the forehead back and forth gently to see what side of the head is a little bit larger or higher. Dr Elsner found that the higher/bigger side was the dominant side. This being the case then the opposite side would be the inherited handed side. For example, if the right brain side of the head was bigger or higher, then the individual would be left-handed from birth. If the left brain side was bigger or higher then they would be right handed from birth.

Sadly, Dr Paul B Elsner passed away in January 2005, at the age of 91. His contribution and research into personology and his knowledge will still be of great practical help to many especially children and the school system. Dr Elsner's small book, "Genetic Testing", has some powerful, straight, hard facts and information about how the school system failed at getting to the root-cause of many learning disabilities.

CHECKING THE HEAD TO ESTABLISH THE HANDEDNESS OF A CHILD

Her right side of head higher. Birth handedness is left.

His right side of head higher. Birth handedness is left.

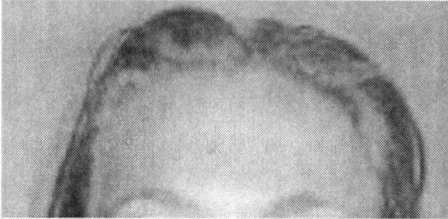

Fig A

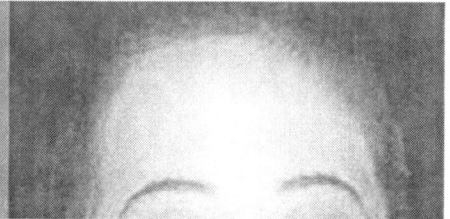

Fig B

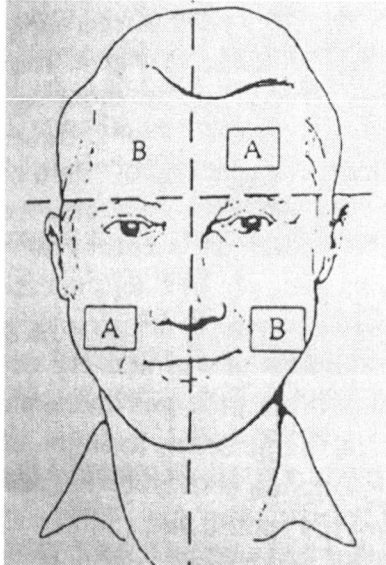

Fig C

Fig C illustrates the cross over point of the brain to the dominant side, either right or left handed.

These examples (Fig A and B) illustrate Dr Elsner's findings. Both these youngsters have a larger right brain and should be, according to Dr Elsner, left-handed. They were, in fact, using their right hand. But what were their writing and mathematics abilities like? The female managed to write to a reasonable degree, but as far as mathematics were concerned, it was a nightmare: she got confused, had mental blocks, was totally mentally frustrated and couldn't focus for long.

The young man had problems with both and couldn't master either. If school teachers check this simple fact and take a look at the heads of all those having real problems with reading and writing, it might surprise them to make this basic observation. It will be interesting to see if further research is carried out in the future, but the overwhelming feedback from the investigation Dr Elsner undertook over the years, leaves us with something to seriously think about, if your child is having learning problems.

Dr Elsner's book, "Genetic Testing", had a complete list of all the traits affecting behaviour in children. The list is enclosed here for reference. As Dr Elsner once said to me (I was also a student of Dr Elsner): "There are no bad traits, there are good traits and traits that are out of control." The following pages list some of the traits found by his research to affect children and youths with regard to education and schools.

CHILDREN'S TRAITS AND EDUCATION

A brief list of traits associated with either a gift or a potential problem with children and youths

Sports and athletic
Traits: Maternal – short -legged, athletic, thick hair, physically motivated.

Leadership qualities
Traits: forceful, authoritative, self -confident, self-reliant, concise.

Musical talent
Traits: music appreciation and pitch, good hand dexterity and coordination.

Writing ability
Traits: rhetoric, imagination, good hand dexterity.

Construction skills
Traits: construction head, good hand dexterity and coordination, thick hair.

Negative traits that need positive redirection to avoid disrupting the flow of learning

Wrong-handedness
Traits: mixed dominance, hand not used according to dominant brain side. If right brain dominant, then the pupil will be left-handed and vice versa.

Differing interests
Traits: interests – people, information, things, may conflict with others.

Time and detail given to a project
Traits: fast/slow thinker, analytical, gullible/trusting and sceptical. The reason why some will hand in work quickly while others take far too long.

Poor quality of work performed
Traits: tolerance, intolerance, critical, uncritical, exacting. Some pupils will have a low score on these traits and not be conscientious about doing quality work.

Approachability or friendly
Traits: affability, discrimination, may get easily side -racked, looking round to talk to someone or may be unfriendly.

Attitude to assignments
Traits: methodical, backward balance, may day-dream in class, forget project and assignment or go off track or be to the other extreme.

Bored with the subject
Traits: fast thinker, interested in things, cannot focus on task not interested in, mind will wander and want to be elsewhere.

Student always upset with his work
Traits: exacting, intolerance, critical, demands to much of themselves.

Identifying the causes
of unacceptable conduct and behaviour

Has poor choice of friends:
Traits: tolerance, non-critical, affable (too friendly).

Will not remain seated in class
Traits: maternal (short-legged), physically motivated, interest in things.

Talks and disrupts the class
Traits: impulsive, tolerant, jovial, verbose, affectionate.

Does not follow school rules
Traits: unconventional, adventurous, tolerant.

Takes and uses others' property
Traits: acquisitive (likes to collect things), unconventional.

Displays a bad temper/tantrums
Traits: forward ego balance, stubbornness.

Displays stubbornness or rebels
Traits: stubbornness, auto-resistance, analytical, intolerance, critical.

Excessive tardiness, lateness, slowness
Traits: tolerance, procrastination, non-competitive.

Homework not completed on time
Traits: tolerant, no tenacity or pugnacity.

Argumentative
Traits: critical, stubbornness.

Takes unacceptable risks
Traits: risk-taking, adventurous.

Does not get along with others
Traits: body Insulation – thick hair, intolerant, critical.

Eating disorders
Traits: melancholy (stress/depression) conservation head, sensitive.

Has no friends
Traits: intolerant, critical, discriminating, low sensitivity/thick hair, direct and forward balance.

Displays selfishness and tantrums
Traits: not affectionate, concise/serious-minded, forward balance.

Overly jealous
Traits: intolerant, serious.

Individuals with special needs that may need extra attention and time

Emotional concerns
Traits: melancholy, depression.

Cruelty and spiteful toward others
Traits: cruelty.

Untrustworthy
Traits: untrustworthy, shifty eyes.

Accident-prone
Traits: melancholy, casualty trend.

Eating disorders
Traits: depression, conservation, temperament, hair thickness.

Violent outbursts and tantrums
Traits: cruelty, intense feelings, thick hair, intolerant, forward balance.

READING FACES - EXAMPLES

Examples of what reading faces will tell you about a person

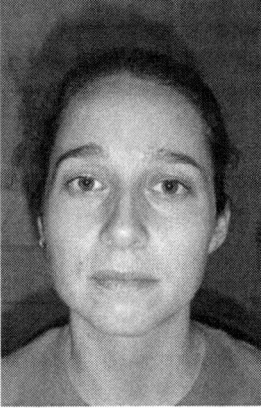

People-friendly and very warm, affectionate nature. Has gift for music and art. Has good imagination and gift for organization. Likes to get things right and is a perfectionist, good at working with hands. Likes information and news. Has high standards and expectations, can be fussy. Not forceful. Talks and gives freely. Very trusting. Can do administrative work. Sensitive and emotional nature could get hurt easily. Has good intuition and original ideas. Can be a little impulsive at times. Outgoing nature. Will make friends easily. Is mentally motivated and likes to think things through first before taking action.

Helpful nature and good working with people but would be better working on projects. Likes information and news. Is career-driven. Has good concentration and needs warning before interrupting him. Very considerate. Tolerant. Analytical and likes to question things and ask why. Patient and will not get upset easily. Very trusting. Will love the challenge of change and new things. Not impulsive. More mentally motivated and will think about things first. Gift for structural and design work. Generous giver. Likes intellectual conversation and projects. Has pioneer trend and will feel desire to work for himself rather than for others. Conscious of self development and improving himself.

Self-reliant and good working on her own with confidence. Very direct and to the point, says exactly what she feels. Tendency to be serious. Mentally motivated. Very generous and kind-hearted, likes to give. Kind nature when dealing with people. Can do administrative work. Optimistic. Is an organized thinker. Very forward balance and likes to think ahead more than to the past. Can be critical and judgemental due her very honest, direct manner. Very tolerant but can be impatient in a moment. Reliable, trustworthy and very dependable. Needs constant re-assurance and security and likes to feel she is secure or she will feel agitated and unsettled.

People-friendly and has the clinically clean look, as seen in medical fields. Is fussy and picky and will tend to spend time on details rather than see the big picture. Will hold feelings in. Concise when talking and to the point. Mentally motivated and has high intellect. Little mean with his money and will spend easily only when he wants. Will tend to be very tidy and neat. When asking questions does not like lengthy explanations and will get agitated if people give lengthy answers. Will want to interrupt them and cut **them** short. Has good mental recall and **original** ideas.

Warm-natured and very people friendly, likes to **talk and** is very generous. Has good **organizational** ability and design appreciation. Is **physically** motivated and restless, needs to **have breaks** and move around. Is little **impatient.** Very sensitive and will tend to take things personally. Is trusting, but can also do administrative and ministrative work. Little fussy and picky. Does not like to waste things. Very emotional and has high eye magnetism and will make friends easily. Has high standards and moderate mood swings. Will tend to get irritated and agitated quickly due to her high standards. She is confident and is an object-thinker (quick).

People friendly. Very confident and has good authority, will want to take charge of situations and be in control. Very tolerant and easy-going, but extremely impatient in a moment. Non-critical, friendly but likes to keep own space and distance when meeting people until confident with them. More mentally motivated and takes things very personally if upset. Personal appearance important. Generous, likes to talk. Can be picky and fussy. Very affectionate. Very forward balanced, maybe bossy, prone to tantrums if she cannot get her own way.

176

People-friendly and loves working with people. Bottom-line person who likes direct answers. Not naturally confident but gains confidence through knowledge. Is more concise and gives direct answers when speaking. Is physically motivated and restless and likes to be on the move. Is very sensitive and emotional toward others. Interested in personal development. Has a more serious nature and takes things seriously. Has dry sense of humour. Can be little stubborn at times and may automatically resist. Has caring nature toward others and very honest.

Has good imagination, is original thinker, very creative. Very sensitive, will be very conscious of her appearance, Has pugnacity and tenacity and can push herself if she wants to. Has critical perception and will spot errors and has good eye for detail. Is people-friendly, will work well in a team. Has design appreciation and gift for creative projects. Has good sense of humour. Will get hurt easily and take things personally. Is backward balanced and thus more considerate and may tend to daydream. Likes peace and order with surroundings.

Is forward balanced and more interested in the present than the past, Is authoritative and very confident. Tougher and will love working outdoors. Is analytical and will like to question things and ask why. Is adventurous. Is tolerant and more laid back. Is very trusting by nature and may have tendency to spend money easily. Interested in projects and things rather than in people; has good intellect. More generous by nature and likes to give or share.

ABOUT THE AUTHOR

I am a certified personologist, born in the UK and have been researching and studying people as a hobby for many years – since I was in my teens, I am now 57 years of age (2008). I also take great interest in body language and observe that the way people walk tells a lot about what is going on in the mind. I started studying face language, face reading or facial genetics known as personology in recent years, particularly after my visit to China where I met several face reading experts. People give away many signs and signals as to how they think and reason and what their true attitude and motives really are. Mannerisms and habits also play a big part in reading what they truly are. In fact some people give off so many signals, they really don't need to tell you anything!

Stand in a supermarket queue and look in the shopping trolleys of customers and you will immediately see what type of person they are – big spenders, wasteful, with poor eating habits, health conscious, homemakers or good time seekers, untidy, fussy – the clues are all there. Even dress and the way they clean their shoes will tell you what they live like at home and give you loads of clues. Take, for example, shoes. I notice this with doctors in hospitals, lawyers and solicitors in courts, that some wanting to make an impression and to sound authoritative wear hard metal tips under the heel and make a lot of noise when stepping along corridors. It sounds, in fact, impressive and does tend to give an impression of authority rather than a soft shoe like a slipper! When looking at the style of walking, these people definitely walk more upright and are somewhat bossier than a soft shoe person. Check it out next time you see or hear heavy footsteps!

Observation then is very important and observing expressions and traits of the face will quickly give you a true picture of the person you are looking at. I have found this to be true so many times and it's a great tool to have. Remember, face traits are one thing, expression is another: put the two together and you can see who is really behind the mask. Forget the make-up, posing and all the other things people hide behind, *the face never lies.*

In the course of my life, I have also studied people in mind-control cults and how the people are manipulated. Even an honest-hearted person with a good education and sound thinking, can easily be pulled into such cults. I also noticed that various types of people have certain traits and found that I became very good at quickly drawing the right conclusions, before they open their mouths, as to what they would be like and the reception I would get when approaching them. I tried this out on thousands of people over the years and became what might be best called "a good judge of character".

Now, after putting all these things together and discovering personology and facial trait reading, I have found this to be extremely accurate. I have been trained under two of the best known teachers in the USA – Naomi Tickle and Dr Paul B Eslner PsD USA. Naomi has been a professional personologist adviser for over 20 years and is a world-renowned expert in face language. She set up the "International Centre of Personology" in San Francisco and is a member of the International Coach Federation. Dr Elsner was a certified personologist and genetic analyst for 60 years under "The Personology Foundation of the Pacific" USA.

Naomi studied Robert Whiteside's work by introduction to his research via his nephew, Bill Whiteside. Robert was a pioneer founder of personology and associate of judge Edward Vincent Jones (USA). Much of the work that we see today was validated by Robert Whiteside who, with his wife Elizabeth, carried out most of the profile research and statistical data. This information is dealt with in Bill Whiteside's book "Nature's Message", for those interested to know more details about the work. Dr Elsner was part of a team involved with the lab assignments research at San Quentin prison and the Air Force recruitment program (USA) to establish the modern foundation and accuracy of personology. Dr Elsner also did work at mental institutions and asylums, working with patients in researching behavioural and demeanour traits.

I am a graduate student of both the International Centre of Personology USA and The Personology Foundation of the Pacific. I use the exact methods pioneered by the late Judge Edward V Jones, the original investigator of genetic traits, facial and head physical features. The measurements are taken using the same instruments Robert Whiteside and Edward V Jones designed as they are simple but effective. Even though some 70 years later, I have found nothing that has been able to match the system for accuracy and I have investigated and talked to a lot of people over the years.

For those wanting to learn more about face reading, I would seriously recommend Bill Whiteside and Naomi Tickle as two of the best experts in this field. Both supply books and courses well worth the investment and study. Dr Elsner has now passed away, but his daughter I believe is carrying on his work.

I wish all those who read and study the information between the covers of this book have success in finding better relationships and bring peace and understanding into their lives, homes and work place. Misunderstanding caused by lack of knowledge can be replaced by tolerance and compassion for others. We should look at others to identify the best of their traits and encourage them to bring the very best out of themselves, so as to contribute to a better world by understanding who we are and why we do the things we do. Always remember, there are no bad traits, only some individuals that have traits out of control.

I hope the constructive advice and suggestions will help many find peace of mind and better communication so that when we look at each other, we only see the true person for the best, their great gifts and potential and encourage everyone to give all their creative abilities to benefit all. Every single person on the planet has amazing gifts and potential, no matter who they are. They have incredible abilities they may not realise they even posses or have inherited. This goes from the professional to the vagrant sleeping on the street. The gifts are there; they just need help to bring out the best out in themselves. Knowing who you are will open a door to new horizons, goals and adventures. You are unique in the universe; no one is like you!

Discover yourself and your potential and the world will be full of sunshine: faces will never look the same from this day forward. One last thing to remember is that a diamond never comes out of the ground cut and sparkling, it is rough, uncut and looks nothing like a diamond. But put into the hands of a skilled diamond cutter, after much painstaking work, the beauty is revealed. People too are like this. Some have amazing traits but they just haven't been directed onto the right path. With a conscious effort, you will see people who were totally out of control become the most incredible individuals you could ever imagine. Offenders and criminals have been helped to become successful in business, financially independent, leaving a life of bitterness behind and walking a path in life which is now meaningful, happy, positive and constructive.

Every single person has traits that are gifts; it is just knowing which ones we have been blessed with and inherited from our family, be it our parents, grandparents or even great grandparents. As they say, every man can become a carpenter but it takes one man six months and another 20 years. One man has a natural gift while the other finds it a real challenge. If you know your gifts, this will save you endless time-wasting, pursuing something you will know could be extremely difficult, when the time could be dedicated to doing something you have a gift for.

We all have the tools and, as stated in the beginning of this book, it's not up to the tools or the wood, but up to the carpenter on what he decides to do with them. Whatever your traits are, you can become a wonderful person; you have amazing gifts. True freedom starts with good education.

My very best wishes and success to all readers.

Richard M Phelan
Certified Personologist

MORE INFORMATION

For further information on **Face Reading** you may be interested to read the following books and publications. Both of these are based on Judge Edward V Jones work and Robert Whiteside's research.

You Can Read A Face Like A Book
by Naomi Tickle

www.thefacereader.com
Professional training courses are also available.

Nature's Message.
by Bill Whiteside

www.ireadfaces.com
Professional training courses are also available.

INDEX

A physical indicator of each trait and how trait affects individual behaviour. See page references for related information.

Page

THE HAIR

THE HEAD

Round or Oval-shaped forehead   122,125

Conservationist, homemaker, likes to re-use things, a maintainer, friendly and likes working with people and likes to looks after things.

Square-shape forehead   122,125

Constructionist, likes a challenge, loves starting new projects, can appear wasteful, likes to start afresh, use new materials, more career-driven, does not like everyday chores or repeated maintenance-type work.

Forehead slopes back (side profile)   122,124

Object thinker, quick reactions, makes quick decisions based on experience, may come across as impulsive, good in crises situations.

Flat vertical forehead   122,123

Sequential thinker, likes to learn step-by-step, hates pressure, needs time to think, may appear slow, does not like last minute changes.

Flat spot in middle of forehead above eyebrows   133-135

Likes information and likes to hold information about projects and things.

Vertical indentation in forehead between eyebrows   133-135

Likes working with things or projects rather than with people.

High forehead   136-137

High intellect, abstract thinkers, prefers intellectual subjects to stimulate the brain, gets irritated with trivial or small talk, can tend to isolate themselves.

Short forehead   136,138

Prefers general information and small talk; trivial and mundane things are the big things in life, may feel uncomfortable with more intellectual conversation, they don't see need for it. Called "soap opera" mentality.

More head in front of ears than the back   84-86

Forward balance, likes to move forward, needs recognition, prone to tantrums/selfishness, "me first" attitude, most important thing in life is themselves, likes to be centre of attention. Low consideration for others.

More head behind ears than the front 84-86

Backward balance, hard to let go and lives in past, tendency to daydream, more considerate, good support worker, does not like being centre of attention. More quiet nature.

Back of head narrower than front 77-78

Low progressive, low competitive drive, reluctant and procrastinates, dreams more than acts – everything is "I will do this later", but later never comes.

Head wider in front of ears than back of ears 77-78

Less competitive, will tend to do things just because they enjoy it, non-competitive, will tend to procrastinate, but has good intentions.

Back of head wider than front 78

Progressive, likes to move on things, a doer rather than thinker, will tend to have lots of drive, wants to get things done, get into the action.

Back of head higher than front 79

Forceful and can come across as pushy, has strong drive to accomplish pursuits, can come across as headstrong or bossy, self-willed.

Front of head higher than back 79

Idealistic, full of ideas but often fails to carry them through, then gets agitated if someone uses their ideas; great inventors and ideas.

Middle of head is higher than front and back 141-142

Completely idealistic, a dreamer, lives in a fantasy world, unrealistic in approaching real-life situations, they dream about how everything should be.

Indent in the side of head by end of eyebrow 65-66

Will come across as tactful, will choose and use words carefully, thoughtful, very diplomatic in approaching situations. Will be discreet.

Round full smooth fore-head no side indentation 65,67

Very direct, says exactly what they think, can be offensive or rude, tactless, sometimes very hurtful, tends to loose friends easily as offensive to others.

Sharp right angle top of forehead (side view)   141,143

Forehead looks like square brick from the side, resolute, not open to new ideas, does not like change, set in their own ways, not accepting others' views on things, does not like to change mind, may have tunnel vision only.

THE EARS

Protruding ears that stick out   105-106

Acquisitive, instinctively asks why! Hears everything, tends to accumulate and hoard things and lives in clutter but good money saver.

Flat looking ears against the side of the head   105,107

Low acquisitiveness, tendency to spend money easily, can be wasteful, if sky jump nose, will amplify trait

Large ear lobes   105,108

Conscientious about personal development, found in men inclined towards gardening interests, more generous in nature.

One ear more forward or back than the other   108

Mood swing in being Indecisive and has problems making decisions, constantly changing his mind, this person will drive you crazy forever changing his mind!

Round outer ear shaped like shell   110

Musical appreciation, natural gift for music, rhythm and sounds.

Outer and inner ear ridge has parallel line shape   110

Has good sense of pitch and sound, if thin will prefer high pitch in sounds, if thick and deep will prefer deeper pitch or sounds.

Ears look high on side in line with nostrils   109

Realistic, down to earth and reasonable, views everything with logic and commonsense.

Low-set ears on side of head in line with nostrils   109

Idealistic, likes to dream, unrealistic and tends to live in fantasy world of their own, prone to make unrealistic decisions. See things only as they think they should be.

One ear higher than the other on the side of the head   **109**

Mood swing about standards; will make an issue one day and let it go the next.

Outer edge of ear has straight, flat-looking appearance   **111**

Hates working for others and prefers to work for themselves, likes a challenge to explore new things. Called the "pioneer trend" trait.

THE FACE

Asymmetry in the face.   **149-155**

Indication of mood swings; if asymmetry is extreme, individual can develop unstable, complex emotions and character; vulnerable to criminal tendencies if not kept under control. Always choose calm surroundings.

Sharp or fine features   **30,63**

Tendency to be picky / fussy, called the clinical look, generally more tidy.

More blunt and rounded features   **30**

Less picky / fussy, prone to be untidy and lax about surroundings.

High, protruding check bones   **49-50**

Adventurous, likes to try new things and challenges, desires to travel and move around, hates being in the same place too long, likes to be on the move.

Narrow or slim face   **60-61**

Not naturally confident, builds confidence through knowledge, always wants to learn more; happy to stay at home rather than travel.

Wide face   **60-61**

High self-confidence, acts on limited knowledge, feels no need to study to get more information, will tend to bluff way through situations.

Shorter lower face from nose to chin   **45-46**

Mentally motivated, thinks before taking any action, may appear to be slow to be motivated due to calculating the cost– "I will have to think about that".

Longer lower face from nose to chin   **45-48**

Physically motivated, will tend to react physically without thinking – act now think later! They will strive into action not even knowing what direction to take. Tend to make decisions based on experience of past, not knowledge.

THE EYEBROWS

High-set eyebrows above the eye lid (seen more in females)   **112-113**

Likes to keep little distance, more discriminating toward others, may appear cold and unfriendly, give appearances of being unapproachable.

Half moon-shaped eyebrows   **112,114**

Mechanical appreciation, gift for seeing how things are put together and work, very creative abilities. Make good project managers.

Upside down "V-shaped" eyebrow   **112-113**

Design appreciation and innate ability to understand how things are designed and how to put them together.

Eyebrows start out at sharp upward angle from top of   **112,115**
nose to outside of forehead

Love for drama, will have flare for many things, and thrives on that big entry; flamboyant and more inclined to be an extrovert.

Low-set straight eyebrows, found mostly in men   **112,115**

Aesthetic appreciation, needs peace and order in life; very friendly, talks to anyone; disorder can make them physically ill; they will talk to everyone.

Eyebrows that slope or curve down and are   **112,114**
longer toward the outer-side

Organisational ability and the need to be organised.

Long full or thick looking eye brows   **112,114**

Indication that the individual has good imagination and personal dreams and goals; has hope and enjoys idealistic thinking.

Short block or square-looking eyebrows   **112,114**

Purely practical and shows they aren't interested in idealistic dreams; mostly found in older people or people who have no purpose in life.

Horizontal prominent ridge above eyebrows 139-140

Methodical, a person of habit, does things by routine, a predictable person; often seen in military personnel or regimented thinking people of habit.

Mounds over the inner eyebrows 139-140

Detail concern, has habitual obsession with detail and getting things right.

One or two vertical lines between eyebrows 139-140

Exactness, developed due to trying to get things exactly right or with absolute precision.

THE EYES

Eye magnetism, rich dark iris, sparkle 91-92

The more sparkling the eye colour, the more magnetic the personality; more sensitive, emotional and responsive to others; family ties important.

Low eye magnetism, pale in colour or dull iris, little sparkle 91-92

Maybe cold, lacks warmth towards others or reluctant to show emotional feelings; will be less family-orientated or wanting to stay close to family.

Eyelids covered with fold of skin (Oriental appearance) 95-96

High-analytical, likes to question everything and ask why. Will get irritated if not enough information is given or explained.

Exposed eyelids visible 95-96

Low analytical. A bottom-line person, likes to get to the point, will tend to cut short your sentences and interrupt. Gets very irritated with lengthy answers, wants to know, what is it, how much, where to get it; that's all.

Close-set eyes 87-88

Low tolerance, quick to react to situations, will get irritated if they see others failing to take action, if also object thinker, inward-slopping forehead with amplify the trait. Will see all the details rather than the big picture.

Wide-set eyes 87,89

High tolerance, more permissive will put up with situations, fails to see serious need to take action or discipline if required, will tend to let everything go, only sees the big picture, tendency to overlook the details.

Width between eyes off centre to nose   87,89

Mixed tolerance, prone to mood swings in tolerance, will be a difficult person to live with. One day will tolerate everything, the next they will not tolerate anything.

Both eyes have different upward angle   95,98

Cat's eyes in appearance but one eye at higher angle. Judgemental, will criticize everything, jumps to conclusions, very insecure and can be paranoid. Extremely difficult to live with, very insecure and finds it hard to find trust in others.

Deep-set eyes   91,93

Serious nature. Will look at everything with serious mind as if everything is a big deal, low humour, seldom smiles.

Inner corners of eyes same level   95,100

Conventional, will easily conform and work well in team, will follow rules and toe the line.

Inner corners of eyes not level; one eye appears lower   95,100

Unconventional, will tend do the complete opposite to others, more judgemental, may find it difficult to conform, but very creative.

Large iris in the eyes   101-102

High emotional expression, will have sympathy for others, warm nature, caring attitude.

Small iris in the eyes   102

Low emotional expression, may appear cold and not concerned, tendency to not want to care about others.

Large pupils   91,102

Emotional and sensitive, very sympathetic and warm nature.

Small pupils   91,102

Lacks emotion and is unsympathetic, may be cold in nature.

Outer corner of eye higher than inner corner   95,97
Non-critical, does not look for faults in others, more easy-going, idealistic, forgiving. The higher the angle the more prone to turn on the tears.

Outer corners of eye drop down   95,97
Critical, will spot every error and mistake, tendency to look for faults and difficult to please; nothing is ever right. A very difficult trait to live with.

White under one or both eyes   38-39
Melancholy, sign of severe depression and stress, will be accident-prone, may also appear glassy-eyed if under stress – called fugacity.

One eyelid drops lower than the other   38-39
Cruelty, may have tendency to enjoy hurting people, can be very spiteful, vindictive or nasty if they choose to be if trait is out of control.

Inner corners of eyes long and pointed down   101-102
Exceptionally sensitive and very emotional; will cry easily.

Crow's feet lines by corner of eye   159
Shows a person of good humour and temperament, they like to see the funny or sunny side of life. Life is always full of sunshine to them.

Two lateral lines under one or both bottom eye lids   103-104
Trait called rhetoric and is the gift for writing. If two vertical lines are also seen looking like # they have gift for languages

THE NOSE

Front of nose and nostrils turned down (side profile)   68,70
Sceptical, will doubt and question everything even if you have all the facts, person will reply "I don't' believe it".

Turned up nose, nostril visible (front profile)   68-69
Very trusting and more gullible, fails to question things, can be taken advantage of easily, the salesman sees them coming!

Concave or sky jump nose (side profile)   **68-69**

Ministrative, naturally likes to serve and help others, will spend money easily and tend to give everything away.

Convex nose (like Roman nose, side profile)   **68-69**

Administrative, will tend to take over and run the show, price orientated and a bargain hunter; wants the best deal, will fight for a bargain.

Wide and flared nostrils   **62-63**

Will come across as being very self-reliant and likes to stand on their own two feet, independent.

Pinched or narrow nostrils   **62-63**

Low self reliance, will want support and hesitant to do things on their own; relies on others, always feels need to seek others' approval

Bulbous nose   **62-63**

Inquisitive and likes to know all the news, general interest in everything, in men it can indicate a tendency to be violent or show aggression.

Sharp pointed nose   **62-63**

Likes to search and dig deep for information with an investigating manner, looks for details, will be picky in temperament.

Boxer's nose, swollen look on bridge of nose   **62-63**

Sign of possible aggression and can be violent, if long space from nose to chin will react physically and usually violent in situations.

THE MOUTH AND LIPS

Long philtrum – space from nose to top lip   **56-57**

Dry sense of humour, prone to be sarcastic and often associated with poor dress sense.

Short philtrum – space from nose and top lip   **56-57**

Takes things personally, sensitive feelings, self-conscious, will keep looking in the mirror checking appearance, very creative, woman are great shoppers!

Thick upper lip   **56-57**

Verbose, likes to talk, more lustful nature, higher imagination.

Top lip much thicker than bottom lip 56-57

High sexual imagination, tendency to succumb to being unfaithful or promiscuous if not controlled.

Thin upper lip 56-58

More concise and will talk with deliberate short sentences, will give straight direct answers. Less imaginative.

Thick lower lip 56-58

Very generous, and will automatically give for whatever reason.

Thin lower lip 56-58

Tendency to be mean or stingy, especially handling money, only gives if a reason to give, often fails to see the need to give to others.

Protruding chin, lips and mouth (side profile) 51-52

Impulsive, will rush into things without thinking, if combined with risk-taking, high tolerance traits will be a real problem!

Lips, mouth and chin receding (side profile) 51-52

Less impulsive, if extreme will need a push as can be negative in approaching things. Does not like confrontations.

One or both sides of mouth turned down 71-72

Pessimistic, negative and may come across like a bucket of ice cold slush on a hot fire; only ever see the problem rather than the solution.

Lines running from nostrils to side of mouth 158

Deeper the line the more emphasis on their expression, deep thought behind words, every word counts.

Teeth appear to turn inward 158

Will tend to hold feelings in and good holding secrets and keeping confidentiality.

Protruding teeth 158

Tendency to tell everyone your secrets, and difficulty in keeping confidentiality.

THE CHIN AND JAW

Long space between chin and nose   **45,47**
Physically motivated and restlessness, acts before thinking, can't sit for
long periods, wants to be on the move, may appear impulsive.

Short distance between nose and chin   **45,46**
Mentally motivated, will think before acting, more calculating, may come
across as a bit slow, but this is how they approach all situations – think
first!

Sharp or pointed chin   **53,54**
Automatic resistance, Stubborn and will automatically resist, doesn't like
being told what to do, needs persuasion to invoke cooperation.

Protruding chin   **53,55**
Tenacity, will push any issue; will not back down.

Receding chin   **53,55**
Inclined to back down when confronted with issues, may lack self control or
restraint.

Wide square-looking chin (below the mouth, not jaw width)   **53,54**
Pugnacity, will fight for a cause, physical fighter or can be mental debater!

Narrow jaw compared to width of face   **60-61**
Less authoritative, may not be taken seriously, posture and attire
important.

Wide jaw compared to face   **60-61**
Appearance of upside bucket face shape, comes across as authoritative
and will naturally want to take charge; can be intimidating to others.

THE NECK

Two lines across front of neck   **40**

Vocal lines, gifted with potential singing and music ability.

THE HANDS

Long index ring finger (compared to first finger)   **33-34**

High risk-taking, other traits will indicate impulsive or calculated risk-taker.

Very long thumbs   **33,36**

Intense feeling, tendency to explosive emotions (Caution - needs to be measured correctly); genetic trait found in the Irish.

Three middle fingers similar length   **33-34**

Good hand dexterity, very good with hand skills, naturally gifted to use hands and more gifted to playing instruments.

Hands have gaps between fingers   **33,35**

More philosophical, likes to search for answers such as the meaning of life, will amplify with age, inclined toward meditation interests.

Two first fingers similar length in comparison with the others   **33,34**

Good hand dexterity and ability to use hands.

Short headline on palms   **33,37**

Also known as solitude line; shorter the line the more time a person needs to themselves.

Long headline on palms   **33,37**

Will want company constantly and not like being on their own.

THE LEGS

Long legs compared to short body or torso **22-24**
Inclined to sit and do sit down jobs, tendency to use transport rather than walk, handedness and dominant traits take after father.

Short legs compared to longer body or torso **22-24**
Prefers to stand and do active jobs on feet; likes to walk and be on the move, handedness and dominant traits take after mother

THE SKIN

Tight skin **30**
Will tend to be very fussy and picky and may appear to have a clinical look.

Loose skin **30**
Prone to be messy, untidy in dress and habits; looser the skin the more lax about their surroundings and personal grooming they will be.

THE BODY TONE

Soft muscle tone and build **31**
Will tend to be soft-natured, sensitive, get hurt or offended easily, more emotional.

Hard muscle tone and build **31**
Will be less sensitive, more unsympathetic and low emotion toward others.

THE VOICE

Sharp or loud voice **31**
Will come across as being authoritative and exert power.

A gentle soft voice **31**
Will reflect the person is kind and sensitive by nature.

PERSONAL NOTES

PERSONAL NOTES

PERSONAL NOTES

PERSONAL NOTES

PERSONAL NOTES

PERSONAL NOTES

PERSONAL NOTES

PERSONAL NOTES

PERSONAL NOTES

PERSONAL NOTES

Other Therapeutic Creative Interests
A new dimension in arts and crafts

In the world of arts and crafts, decorative and ornate rope work has so many potential applications. With just a little imagination, one can create some wonderful, eye catching articles. We present an award winning tutorial 94 min DVD with 23 menus to teach you how to make incredible things from rope or cord. **"Knots Made Easy - The Art of Decorative Ropework"** has received over 20 top reviews and was given a presentation award from the Mayor at one of the UK yearly maritime shows for its displays and presentation work. Visit the website and check out some of the amazing things made using this step-by-step tutorial. Print out **FREE** fact sheets of how to get started and ideas of things to make. This tutorial is used by the UK sea cadets and was given commendation from both the "Duke of Edinburgh Award Scheme" UK and the headquarters of the UK "Boy Scouts". Obtain your copy today online.

Free Post and Package worldwide – copy protected.

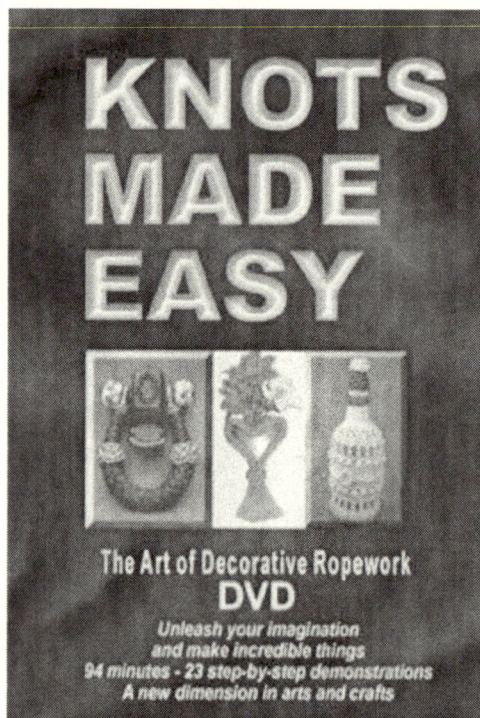

KNOTS MADE EASY

The Art of Decorative Ropework
DVD
Unleash your imagination
and make incredible things
94 minutes - 23 step-by-step demonstrations
A new dimension in arts and crafts

www.knotsdvd.com

Examples of articles made using knots
demonstrated on the DVD

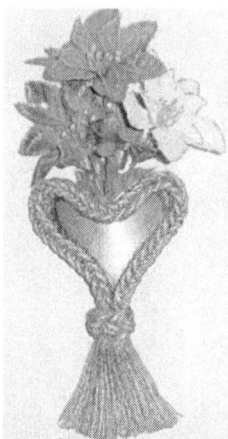

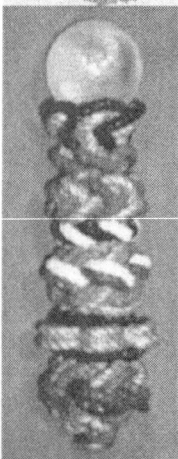

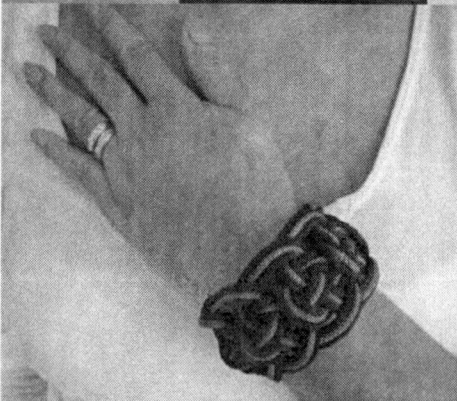
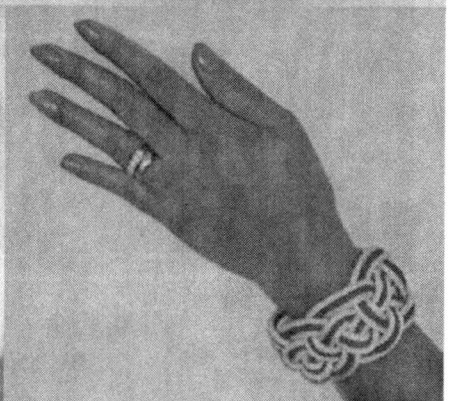

Printed in the United Kingdom
by Lightning Source UK Ltd.
135126UK00003BA/67-147/P